TOWARD AN ADULT CHURCH

A VISION OF FAITH FORMATION

Jane E. Regan, Ph.D.

LOYOLAPRESS.

CHICAGO

LOYOLAPRESS.

3441 N. Ashland Avenue
Chicago, Illinois 60657
(800) 621-1008

Cover Design: Tracey Harris
Interior Design: Becca Taylor Gay and Lucy Lesiak Design

Library of Congress Cataloging-in-Publication Data
Regan, Jane E.
    Toward an adult church : A Vision of faith formation / Jane E. Regan.
        p. cm.
    Includes bibliographical references and index.
    ISBN 0-8294-1806-7
    1. Catholic Church—Adult education. 2. Faith development. I. Title.

BX921 .R43 2002
268' .434—dc21   2001038519

ISBN: 0-8294-1806-7

02 03 04 05 Bang 5 4 3 2

We are told repeatedly
that parents are their children's
first teachers in the faith.
But perhaps we have forgotten
that the converse is true as well.

To
Natalya and Catie

who have taught me a great deal about
what it means to be a woman of faith.

CONTENTS

ACKNOWLEDGMENTS

One spring day, when it was barely spring in Minnesota, I was invited to a meeting of people I knew gathered around a kitchen table in the rectory of the parish I had come to call home. I knew these people. But I did not know that their conversation, and the ones that were to follow, would fundamentally change the way in which I thought about and taught about the activity of catechesis. As spring moved into summer that year and meeting followed meeting (Do you call it a meeting when you sit around in shorts and sip iced coffee and laugh as you figure out how to divide into discussion groups people who don't even know they are coming yet? I don't think so!), there developed a process—really a way of being a parish—that invited all into the movement of faith formation. And so, these days, as the parish of St. Paul's in St. Cloud, Minnesota, brings to conclusion its tenth season of GIFT (Growing in Faith Together), I celebrate with them (from a distance) the energizing force that this has been for them, and cheer for the way it has enriched my understanding of faith formation and called me to a deepening of faith. And so, first, to the people of the Parish of St. Paul, I acknowledge my gratitude and thanks.

And while lots of people have moved in and out of various positions in the parish, the people who shaped the program in the early years and set it on a firm path include Pat Pyle, Chris

Erickson-Thomke, Chris Reicher, Lloyd Haupt, Pat Marech, Vicki Lopez-Kaley, Cathy Sauer, and Tim Baltes. A special thanks to Mimi Bitzan, whose energy and insights were so significant in bringing the ideas and hopes of the parish to life. Her friendship and support are my most treasured gifts. These people and the people of St. Paul's are present in these pages.

In addition, my colleagues at the Institute for Religious Education and Pastoral Ministry at Boston College have my thanks and gratitude as they have supported me in my work and my writing. Special acknowledgment goes to Thomas Groome who has read and critiqued most of the book and to Colleen Griffith and Bud Horell who listened to my chapter variations even as they engaged in their own research and writing. John Paul Sheridan has given a careful editor's eye to my writing; his gift for noting the missing comma does not take away from his ability to see the big picture.

And to my students: the undergrads who have asked "So what?" and the MA students who have asked "What's next?" and the doctoral students whose questions and interests and energy have pushed me to think beyond my own meaning perspectives—thank you!

A good deal of what appears in these pages has come to light in classes I've taught or workshops I have given. My gratitude goes to all of the people who have jogged my thinking with their insights and have encouraged me to keep at it with their affirmations.

The people at Loyola Press have served as a helpful and challenging forum for exploring many of the ideas examined in this book and their implications for parish life. Particular thanks go to Barbara Campbell, Jim Campbell, and Dan Gast as well as to Louise Howe, who served as editor for the book. Having colleagues who both affirm the vision and yet stay rooted in the reality of Church today is a gift that every minister and educator treasures—I know that I do!

And to my family—my mother and sister, my brothers and their families: I have been grateful for your support. And my wonderful daughters who learned at an early age to ask "Are you working at home today?" rather than "Do you have the day off?"—my expressions of gratitude for your presence in my life can never be enough.

May 13, 2001
Fifth Sunday of Easter
and Mother's Day

Jane E. Regan

ABBREVIATIONS

ACCC   International Council on Catechesis, *Adult Catechesis in the Christian Community*

AG   Vatican Council II: *Decree on the Church's Missionary Activity (Ad gentes)*

ChL   John Paul II, *Apostolic Exhortation on the Vocation and the Mission of the Lay Faithful in the Church and in the World (Christifideles Laici)*

CT   John Paul II, *Apostolic Exhortation on Catechesis (Catechesi Tradendae)*

EN   Paul VI, *Apostolic Exhortation on Evangelization (Evangelii Nuntiandi)*

GCD   Congregation for the Clergy, *General Catechetical Directory* (1971)

GDC   Congregation for the Clergy, *General Directory for Catechesis* (1997)

GS   Vatican Council II, *Pastoral Constitution on the Church in the Modern World (Gaudium et Spes)*

OHWB   National Conference of Catholic Bishops, *Our Hearts Were Burning Within Us: A Pastoral Plan for Adult Faith Formation in the United States*

RCIA   Rite of Christian Initiation of Adults

RM   John Paul II, *On the Church's Missionary Mandate (Redemptoris Missio)*

INTRODUCTION

The coming of May marks the conclusion of formal programs of religious education for most parishes. Program coordinators and catechists give a collective sigh of satisfaction as another year is brought to a successful conclusion. Books are stacked, crayons and pencils and paper are sorted, and supplies are stored in readiness for next year's program.

In many parishes a meeting for evaluation and planning takes place. Perhaps it proceeds like this: Toward the end of May, the director of religious education, one or two of the key coordinators, and the pastor gather to evaluate the past year's program and to begin making plans for the following year. The conversation is a lively one with positive comments about the dedication of the volunteers. It is noted that some program changes from the prior year led to an increased level of attendance and engagement on the part of some of the learners. And those involved in leadership are generally pleased with the level of participation in the various liturgical experiences. Although it is seen as a good year, some concerns are also raised. A few of these could be addressed with a bit of added attention—beginning and ending on time, for example, and better communication with those who did not attend a given session. Other concerns reflect perennial uneasiness: What is the best response to those who take exception to the content or to the way in which the content is presented? How does a parish effectively celebrate initiation sacraments—Baptism, Eucharist, and Confirmation—as parish events?

I

Once the evaluation is completed, discussion turns to the plans for next year. Calendars are brought out and the beginning of each liturgical season is noted. Schedules are drawn up and reworked and tentatively set out; they will be coordinated with the proposed calendars from other aspects of parish life with some hope of minimizing schedule conflicts in the coming year. Questions concerning the formation of volunteers for the next year's program are explored. Ideas for potential resources are proposed and considered.

At the end of the day, the group gathered has set the course for next year's program, and the members of the group have, at some level, rededicated themselves to religious education in the parish and to the faith formation of the participants.

That process of bringing one year to completion and projecting the hopes for the next happens with various levels of success and intentionality in parish after parish, large and small. The gathering in the small rural parish, with a pastor who has responsibility for two or three other parishes, might be simply the volunteer coordinator and the pastor meeting in the office of a small rectory on one of the two afternoons a week when the pastor is in the parish. In the large suburban parish the group might be a dozen full-time or part-time professionals gathering in one of the nicely appointed meeting rooms in the parish center. Almost anyone involved in religious education can picture meetings similar to the one described here and can easily list the topics discussed and the concerns raised.

In the majority of parishes, at most of the evaluation and planning meetings, the focus of the conversation is the faith formation of children and youth. The positive comments about the dedicated volunteers might revolve around the great team of catechists that worked with the fourth graders on a special project. Perhaps the new model for the seventh graders that involved them in service opportunities was met with some level of enthusiasm on the part of the youth: that is worth affirming! And perhaps this year the link between catechesis and liturgy was really evident in the way in which the second graders and their families entered into the monthly liturgies that enhanced the sacramental formation program. These elements of a parish program are appropriately highlighted and affirmed; they are signs of a vital engagement with the process of forming the faith of the young people of the parish.

The concerns raised at the meeting also focus on the religious education of children and youth. Perhaps over the course of the year some parents within the parish repeatedly expressed their fear that their children "aren't learning the basics" or that catechists are straying from the book. Or perhaps this was the year the decision was made to move the celebration of First Eucharist to the regular Sunday liturgies and the heat from that decision has not yet fully cooled. Whatever the affirmation, whatever the concerns, the point of emphasis of the evaluation is on the religious education of children and youth. That is where the focus of the program rests.

The planning dimension of these meetings focuses on scheduling the weekly grade-level classes so that there is no conflict with school holidays, there is time for catechists to meet, and there are at least twenty-five sessions for each grade. Once the overall schedule is designed around the school year, the liturgical year is given some acknowledgment. Plans for Advent wreaths, Epiphany celebrations, and Lenten calendars are placed into the schedule at appropriate points. The planning for catechist formation begins with a list of "returning" and "not returning" catechists and then the names of possible volunteers to fill the empty spots are compiled. The resources under consideration are generally contained in the fairly complete "packages" offered by the major textbook publishers. The discussion for next year revolves around keeping or switching series and deciding which of the "extras"—videos, CDs, workbooks, parent pages—are worth purchasing.

At the end of the day, the participants have moved ahead one more year the model that has taken pride of place in our parishes during the last half of the twentieth century and completely set aside—either intentionally or by default—the possibility of a different future for faith formation within the parish.

ADJUSTING THE FOCUS

But what would it be like if we shifted the focus of attention from children and youth to adults? What would be the potential effect on these evaluation and planning meetings if the "learners" being considered were not first graders or fourth graders or tenth graders, but adults? How would the comments and concerns change? What would be the themes of the affirmations and challenges? Without neglecting the former, what would it be like if adult catechesis were allowed to define the catechetical paradigm? How would the discussion of schedule and volunteers and resources shift if the first question asked centered on the faith formation of the adult community and in light of that, the faith formation of the children and youth?

That is the perspective proposed and examined in this book. At the heart of my proposal is an effort to uncover the implications and impact of shifting the locus of the collective attention of religious educators from children and youth to adults. What would be the impact on parish life, on the understanding of faith formation, on the fundamental notion of the place of faith in the life of the believer if the lens we pick up when we begin evaluating and planning religious education efforts at the parish and regional levels brings into clear focus the needs and concerns of the adult community?

This book is addressed to the theorist and practitioner of religious education who is attempting to establish a framework for adult catechesis as well as a balanced approach for bringing it to the center of parish life. In Part One, consideration is given to the core issues that come into play as we speak of the centrality of adult catechesis. It begins with an exploration of the rationale for this renewed attention on the faith life of the adult community. What is meant by adult faith formation in service to an adult church (Chapter 1)? Chapter 2 examines the nature of adult faith and the process of meaning making at the heart of adult life.

Part Two draws on the resources of adult education theory both to set out the philosophical framework and to examine some methodological issues which are applicable to education within a faith context (Chapters 3 and 4).

Bringing the insights from Parts One and Two together, the focus in the third part of the book is on the expression of adult formation within the faith community. Attention is given to establishing principles whereby various opportunities for engaging the adult community can foster genuine adult growth (Chapter 5). Implications for catechist formation and for the ways in which leadership engage the community in the process of embracing an alternative vision of religious education are examined (Chapters 6 and 7). How does parish leadership facilitate a community in the process of embracing this understanding of faith formation with the focus on adults?

I am convinced that the vitality of our parishes and the Church's capacity to fulfill its mission of proclaiming the reign of God are dependent on a refocusing of our energy and resources to the ongoing faith life of adults. I am also convinced that there is recognition and growing interest of the need to rethink catechesis. My hope is that this book will contribute to this essential shift.

PART ONE

SETTING THE FOUNDATIONS

WHAT WOULD IT MEAN TO PICK UP THE LENS OF RELIGIOUS education and shift its focus from the catechesis of children and youth to the catechesis of adults? What would come into clearer focus? What would recede a bit to the back or side? What would be the implications of this for how we plan, execute, and evaluate religious education in our parishes? What are the core themes that need to be brought into the conversation in order to examine this proposal?

Have you ever tried to French braid the hair of a five year old? Dividing the mass of hair into the appropriate strands and actually getting the first few plaits in place are difficult enough. But then, just as a smooth rhythm is established, more hair needs to be added in and integrated into the braiding process. And never mind that the five year old is shifting in her seat, anxious to get on with the day! The end result is seldom as neat as imagined; stray strands and short ends halo the braid, waiting for the first breeze to set them free as the five year old dashes for the door.

Naming what it means to move toward an adult Church is something like trying to French braid a five year old's hair. The multiple strands that make up the reality of an adult Church can be separated for the sake of analysis, but their fundamental interconnection needs to be maintained for the sake of the whole. No one strand can stand on its own in revealing the nature of the movement toward an adult Church, and the weaving together of the various perspectives is never easy or smooth.

To some extent, this book is about weaving together the various elements that are at the heart of being and becoming an adult Church. Themes introduced in one chapter will find echoes and connections with those in other contexts. In Part One, I set out the first two foundational themes. First we look to the call that has been present in church documents since Vatican Council II and explore the rationale for saying that all catechesis is oriented toward adults. In order to do this, we need to examine in some detail the call to evangelization and the challenge to be an evangelizing church. Second, I examine what it means to be an adult and draw out the insights from theology and the social sciences that help to define the movements of adult faith.

The foundations for forming an adult church are an understanding of the mission of the church and a sense what it means to give expression to a mature faith.

1

TOWARD AN ADULT CHURCH

❖

Consider this analogy: A photographer approaches her subject with care and attention to the whole image. She may walk around a scene, exploring angles and examining perspectives: she notes the way the light hits, the complementarities of colors, the juxtaposition of size and depth. As she approaches the moment of photographing, she has in mind an intention for the picture: she knows at some level what she wants this picture to convey, what image she hopes will catch the eye and attention of the viewer. As she brings the camera to her eye, she adjusts the lens, bringing into clear relief the focal point of her picture. Other elements stand in complementary relationship to this point of convergence. The picture would not be complete without the background, without the other figures or images. But their meaning and depth are interpreted in relationship to the point of focus.

Another photographer comes upon the same scene. As he examines the contours and explores the elements of the whole, his imagination brings into focus an alternative picture. His point of reference—the image he is attempting to capture—is different from the first photographer's. As he raises the camera to his eye, he brings into focus another element of the picture, one that had been in the background of the prior shot. The image that had been in the background before is now in focus, other elements are still in the picture, but are perceived differently in relationship to the new focal point.

While one could say that the two resulting photographs are pictures of the same thing, the sense they convey could be quite different. All the components are present in both pictures, but they are perceived and interpreted differently in relationship to the focal point of the photograph.

A similar dynamic is being proposed here as we look at the reality of religious education. The "picture" of religious education in most parish settings and, indeed, in the common consciousness of the Church at large, has as the focal point children and youth. The children and youth stand in clear focus, often in the center of the picture. Framing them are the adults within the community who have responsibility for their faith formation: these would include teachers and catechists, pastor and catechetical leadership, and parents as well. Various elements of the life of the parish are visible in the distance. Serving as background for this particular picture of religious education are the general life and ethos of the community, the liturgical life of the parish, the level of relationship among the members, the place of social action, as well as other parish structures or organizations. Each of these would be relatively clear or fuzzy, located toward the center or periphery of the picture, depending on the perspective of the religious education leadership. But all of them would be viewed in light of the focus of the endeavor—children and youth.

Just as in a photograph, if we shift the locus of attention for religious education, other elements within the broader picture will be seen in a new light and from a new perspective as well. What had been at the periphery of the picture might move more toward the center; elements that had been seen in a supporting role might become more significant. And dynamics that had been central might be viewed from a somewhat different angle. While the elements included in this newly composed "picture" of religious education are the same, their role and significance are seen from a new perspective in light of the shift in focus.

As it stands right now, in most settings the prime question asked in thinking about and planning for catechesis within the parish community is What do the children and youth need to continue to grow in their faith? A secondary question may involve looking to the adults in the community, but that question is often expressed in terms of children and youth: What do the adults need in order to enhance the formation of their children and youth? I am proposing that the prime question be changed in order to focus on adults. We might begin with a question like: What do the adults within the community need in order to grow in their faith? While this might appear to simply replace one group (children and youth) with another (adults), at the core of this book is the conviction that fostering the faith of the adults within a community has the effect of creating a context that supports the life of faith of everyone in the community.

Shifting the focal point or the prime question asked of religious education from children and youth to adults involves realigning the elements of the broad picture of religious education. In doing this we are invited to ask about the elements that contribute to the faith formation of the entire parish community: adults as well as children and youth. Shifting the focal point does not drop elements out of the picture all together; it sets them in a different context and into a different set of relationships. Shifting the focal point from children and youth to adults does not mean dropping children and youth from the picture; it means setting the very important work of the faith formation of children and youth into a broader and more substantive framework. Once the first question (What does the adult community need in order to be an adult church?) is examined, a secondary question emerges, What do the children need to know, to experience, to understand so that they can engage ever more fully in the life of an adult church as they grow and mature?

In some way the question, What does the adult community need in order to be an adult church? is also a response to the earlier question, What do the adults need in order to enhance the formation of their children and youth? In the final analysis, adults enhance the faith life of the children and youth by giving expression to an adult faith; by being an adult church.

In many religious education programs, the formation of children and youth is done in isolation from the faith community. Tucked away on a Tuesday or Wednesday afternoon, the programs have little effective connection with the life of the community, with the liturgical life of the parish, with the way in which the parish gives expression to its faith in action for justice. To bring the focus of the religious education from children and youth to adults is to realign the picture in such a way that the dynamic reality of parish life, lived out by the adults, serves as an essential framework and foundation for the faith formation of children and youth. The shift in focus to adults does not denigrate the religious education of the coming generation; it sets that task within an effective and sustaining framework—the whole faith community.

Taking a New Picture

My proposal is not simply to reinvigorate the present configuration of religious education with its focus on children and youth; the proposal here is to reimagine the religious education endeavor from the perspective of the faith formation of the adult community and, in light of that, the formation of children and youth.

A variety of reasons can be set forth for why this shift in the focus of the "picture" of religious education is an important and even essential one. I suggest two key components of the overarching rationale: First, the present model cannot adequately address the essential dimensions of the catechetical enterprise. And, second, to be genuinely Church in the twenty-first century, a dedication to fostering mature, committed adult communities of faith is essential.

A classic in the field of religious education exposed a fundamental fault line in the present configuration of religious education almost twenty-five years ago. In *Will Our Children Have Faith?* John Westerhoff looked critically at the "schooling-instructional paradigm" of religious education, which was dominant in Protestant and Roman Catholic circles at the time and still prevails today.[1] Foundational to his critique of the schooling-instructional model is its separation from the other formative elements of the life of the faith community. Westerhoff wrote of this as a "broken ecology." The other elements of community life that had supported the instructional dimension—a homogeneous community, a secure and extended family, schools, the parish as social context—are no longer present. Because of this, the schooling model has been required to take the weight of the formation that had in the past taken place in the ebb and flow of the faith community and neighborhood life.

It is not the schooling-instructional paradigm per se that Westerhoff is critiquing. The regular gathering of children and youth in peer groups to learn the stories and mores of the community, to gain the skills and knowledge needed to be engaged members of the community is essential. What Westerhoff is questioning is the isolation of these peer groups from the communal, liturgical, and social justice of the community. The best of instruction about the life of the community, the role of ritual, and the call for social justice cannot replace an experience of community life, engagement with the liturgical life of the church, and active involvement in action for justice.

Westerhoff's challenge that religious educators situate the schooling-instructional model within the broader context of the various elements of parish life applies still in the present. Much of his work subsequent to *Will Our Children Have Faith?* has focused on expanding the scope of catechesis and establishing links between catechesis and liturgy and between catechesis and the socializing effect of community life. It must be noted, however, that with his earlier work and continuing with some nuance into his more recent writing, Westerhoff's focus is primarily on the formation of children and youth.[2] In that context, one could argue that the schooling-instructional model serves as a central, though not comprehensive, element of catechesis. However, it is important to examine the appropriateness of that model when the focus of catechesis shifts to adults. Many of the presumptions of the schooling-instructional paradigm—the role of the teacher, the place of content, and the primary goals, for example—are less helpful in reference to the catechesis of adults.[3]

So, how do we speak of the dynamics of catechesis in such a way as to articulate an essentially adult perspective while acknowledging the place of children and youth? Looking not so much at approach or model (e.g., schooling model), but looking instead at a fundamental description of the nature of catechesis, serves as a helpful starting place.

A reading of ecclesial documents on catechesis that have been published over the past thirty-plus years gives evidence of the expanding understanding of the nature of catechesis and its place in the life of the Church.[4] The most recent documents on both the universal and the national level—the *General Directory for Catechesis* and *Our Hearts Were Burning Within Us*, respectively[5]—speak of catechesis as one of the most important ecclesial activities (*GDC* 29). It is seen as an essential moment of evangelization[6] and has as its aim "to put people not only in touch, but also in communion and intimacy, with Jesus Christ" (*GDC* 80). The *Directory* gives the image of catechesis as an apprenticeship that lasts a lifetime!

Apprentices come to "know" their trade on a number of levels. On one level there is information to gain—the carpenter's apprentice learns the details of types of wood, the way in which trees grow, and the best way to smooth a plank. At the same time, the carpenter's apprentice is formed into the way of carpentry: how to think about the various tools, how to become part of the larger group of carpenters, how to recognize and appreciate fine craft-work. And finally, over time and with increasing depth, the apprentice becomes a carpenter—the apprentice is transformed in how she thinks about herself and her world and takes on the perspective of a carpenter. The "knowing" that is the focus of the carpenter's apprentice is a knowing that informs, forms, and transforms. For the Christian, the apprenticeship includes these same dimensions—catechesis is to inform, form, and transform. This threefold understanding of catechesis is reflected in Church documents as well as in the writings of significant religious education theorists. One who has consistently articulated this most clearly is Thomas Groome. In examining the purpose of Christian catechesis, Groome writes:

> Catechists must intend that people come to know their faith at the depth of their very souls. This will be a "knowing" that informs, forms and transforms people in Christian faith. Reaching beyond what the *GDC* calls "mere information," catechesis should enable participants to comprehend and embrace Christian teachings with conviction, to allow such convictions to shape their identity and holiness of life, and their commitment to forge God's reign in the world.[7]

Catechesis *informs* in all of the ways in which the heart and meaning of the Christian message and the church's tradition are presented in a manner that is meaningful in this time and place. Through the informing dimension of catechesis, the learners gain the skills and information to be active members of the Christian community. The term "Catholic literacy" comes to mind here: learning the vocabulary and prayers and people as the foundations of the shared conversations that make a community of faith possible.

Catechesis *forms* in all the ways that people are shaped into the way of life of the believers. The rhythm of anticipation (Advent), remembering-conversion (Lent), and new beginnings (Easter-Pentecost) is designed to shape the perspective of the believer. The calendar of faith (beginning with Advent) is as valid and formative as the fiscal year (beginning in July), the academic year (beginning in September), or the secular calendar (beginning in January). In powerful ways the members of a community are formed in the very rhythm of the community. They are formed by the implicit curriculum of who leads, how decisions are made, where money is spent. The null curriculum of what the community does not talk about, who is not seen gathering with the community, also shapes the believers in the way of this community of faith.[8] The formative dimension of catechesis takes place in all the formal and informal ways in which the community of faith gathers as Church.

Catechesis *transforms* on a number of different levels. As it affords the opportunity for learners to reflect on the source and reasons for belief, and as it provides a context for learners to make the connection between the tradition and their lives, catechesis transforms the learners into believers who are ever more aware of the power and implications of the Gospel in their lives. At the same time, catechesis offers the possibility for members of the faith community to gather in conversation with the potential of renewing and transforming the community's self-understanding of what it means to be Church in a particular time and place. And catechesis includes the call to be about transforming the interactions and structures of society in light of Gospel convictions.

Inform, form, and transform: these three dimensions are complementary and interrelated. While it is possible to separate them here for the sake of discussion, they are inextricably connected. Maintaining these three in a dynamic and intentional relationship is essential for effective catechesis.

For the most part, the models that dominate contemporary religious education have as the first and often primary (sometimes all but exclusive) focus to inform; and usually to inform children and youth. To some extent, that focus is a reasonable one: it is important to foster in children and youth an appropriate level of literacy about the faith, familiarity with the sacred texts, and understanding of the community's rituals and rules. And clearly, each time children gather in peer groups, formation takes place as well. The way the community of learners gathers, who gathers, and how the time is spent are all ways in which the children begin to learn the perspective, the worldview of the wider community of faith. But the link between the community of learners who gather for catechesis and the faith community that serves as its context is seldom effectively made or experienced by the learners. In addition, the work of being able to step back from one's beliefs and the perspective of the community in order to name and appraise their foundation and presumptions—a step necessary to the process of transforming[9]—is clearly beyond the capacity of children and can only be fostered over time and with the attainment of a certain level of cognitive ability. The effective, dynamic integration of all these dimensions can only develop over time.

Even carried out effectively, a model of religious education that ends with early adolescents cannot effectively integrate these dimensions. Good and important foundations can be set, but the full work of catechesis is an adult activity. The present approach often fails to recognize the breadth of the formation life of the faith community and tends to isolate the information element from the other necessary component parts of catechesis. Even in those many contexts where it is done effectively, the exclusive attention to children and youth truncates the potential of the dynamic interrelationship of the work of catechesis to inform, form, and transform.

Simply arguing that the present models are not as effective as they could be would not necessitate a complete change in focus; it could be addressed with an adjustment of the present picture. Being more intentional in connecting the peer group sessions with other aspects of the life of the parish, highlighting the essential link between catechesis and liturgy, and engaging the learners in experience of action for justice would enhance the present model and address some of the core theoretical and practical problems. The discussion thus far might not require or necessarily support the shift in the prime questions asked in planning and evaluating programs of religious education from What do we do with children and youth? to What does the adult community need in order to be an adult church? The impetus for this shift rests in the second component to the overarching rationale—for the church to be genuinely church in the twenty-first century, a rededication to fostering mature, committed adult communities of faith is essential.

Behind this conviction is the issue of a fundamental ecclesiology and understanding of the mission of the church. Catechesis is always in service to an ecclesiology. Whether that ecclesiology is articulated or not, whether the link is intentionally examined or not, our approach to catechesis and our understanding of its goals point to presumptions about the nature of the church.

A premise at the heart of this book and inherent to the understanding of catechesis set out here is that fundamentally the church exists in order to further the kingdom, or reign, of God. People gather into the church in order to be sent out by the Spirit in service to God's reign in human history. There is a dynamic relationship between the church's inner life and its outer work. On the one hand, the church is a gathering of people dedicated to fostering a sense of community among themselves, to expressing that community in worship, and to enhancing the ongoing faith life of the members so that each continues to mature in his or her relationship with God in Jesus Christ. On the other hand, there is the church's task to be an active participant in the work of bringing to life the reign of God. Through the witness of its corporate life and the life of its members, the church proclaims and furthers the reality of God's presence in the "here and now."

Maintaining the complementarities of these elements of the church is essential to catechesis. It is about furthering both the community of faith and the faith life of the members as well as enhancing the potential of the community to further the reign of God. At a fundamental level, catechesis is not only (or even primarily) in service to membership within a particular expression of Christianity. It is also in service to discipleship, the ability to live and make decisions, in light of the Gospel and the reign of God.

We can explore this vision of catechesis more closely by examining the understanding of evangelization that has developed in the church's self-understanding over the past thirty-five years or so, and then tracing out the fundamental link between evangelization and the necessity of adult faith formation.

EVANGELIZATION AND THE CALL FOR ADULT FAITH FORMATION

Writers of ecclesial documents over the past thirty-five years have declared with increasing persistence the centrality of adult faith formation to the catechetical enterprise and the life of the church. Browse through almost any recent document, and you can find a citation that refers back to the 1971 *General Catechetical Directory* and the statement that "catechesis of adults, since it deals with persons who are capable of an adherence that is fully responsible, must be considered the chief form of catechesis. All the other forms, which are indeed, always necessary, are in some way oriented to it."[10] Over this same period of time, ecclesial documents have also been attending with growing clarity to the church's mission to evangelize. Beginning at the time of Vatican Council II and reflected in the council's documents, the concept of "evangelization" has risen to the surface of Catholic consciousness as a way to speak about the fundamental work of the church. In some of the most recent church writings these two strands—the call for adult faith formation and the challenge of evangelization—have coalesced, and their mutual interrelationship has become clear: the work of evangelization requires a mature faith community made possible by the ongoing work of adult faith formation.

For many the term *evangelization* is problematic, bringing with it images of activities more common to some aspects of Protestant traditions—some TV evangelists with their high-pressure "sell" of their own interpretation of the Gospel come to mind. It is important, however, to articulate the difference between proselytizing and evangelizing. In the case of proselytizing, the believer is primarily engaged in preaching with the message focused on telling the other what he or she should believe. Often, those who don't share the faith convictions of the believer experience proselytizing as oppressive. In the case of evangelizing, the believer is engaged in giving expression to his or her beliefs in all of the day-to-day activities that shape one's life. When words are called for, the believer talks about what he or she believes rather than telling others what they should believe. One of the surest signs of evangelization is that it is experienced as liberating rather than oppressing. The goal of proselytizing is bringing in new members; the goal of evangelizing is the furthering of the reign of God: "bringing the Good News into all the strata of humanity, and through its influence transforming humanity from within and making it new."[11]

While the term *evangelization* may have some negative effective history, it is my contention that it is both possible and necessary to reclaim the term for the sake of refocusing our understanding of the mission of the church and the role of adult catechesis. That reclaiming is facilitated by examining the way in which the understanding of evangelization has developed in church documents over the past thirty-five years. These documents serve as stepping stones in tracing the movement from an earlier notion of evangelization as something done to non-Christians by missionaries in foreign lands to the rich and challenging image of the whole Church being called to evangelize. Each of the documents contributes core insights or ideas that enhance our understanding of evangelization.

The Vatican Council II *Decree on the Church's Missionary Activity (Ad gentes),*[12] promulgated in 1965, states clearly that the proclamation of the Gospel to all peoples is at the heart of the Church's mission. But this is not a proclamation in word alone—the witness of the Christian life, the formation of community, and the preaching of the Gospel make up the foundation of evangelization. In addition, the document clearly articulates that evangelization recognizes and enhances the connection between the Gospel and the human situation in history. Multiform in nature, the work of evangelization—missionary activity—is always "intimately bound up with human nature and its aspirations" (*AG* 8).

This conviction that evangelization is concerned with the whole of human life and the whole of human liberation is reflective of the perspective that shaped the deliberation of many of the documents of Vatican II. It was expressed clearly in the opening paragraph of the *Pastoral Constitution on the Church in the Modern World (Gaudium et Spes).* "The joys and hopes, the grief and anguish of the people of our time, especially of those who are poor or afflicted, are the joys and hopes, the grief and anguish of the followers of Christ as well. Nothing that is genuinely human fails to find an echo in their hearts" (*GS* 1). The assumption of the intimate connection between human existence and the saving work of God in Christ serves to open up the understanding of evangelization. It is no longer simply understood as something we do to others or something that we give to others. Evangelization takes on a richer texture and points not only to what we do but who we are with and for others.

In 1975, some ten years after the Council and a year after the Synod on Evangelization, Pope Paul VI issued the *Apostolic Exhortation on Evangelization (Evangelii Nuntiandi).* A key contribution of this document to our understanding of evangelization is its affirmation that evangelization is at the heart of the Church's mission and identity: "Evangelization is in fact the grace and vocation proper to the Church, her deepest identity.

She exists in order to evangelize" (*EN* 14). This document articulates clearly and repeatedly that the entire Church is responsible for evangelization, not simply the officially designated
"evangelizers" or "missionaries." This call to evangelize is both
a corporate one and one shared by each member of the Church.

The relationship between evangelization and catechesis is
central to the 1977 *Apostolic Exhortation on Catechesis (Catechesi Tradendae)*. In that document, evangelization is presented as
a rich and dynamic reality made up of various moments that
must be seen in relationship with one another. Catechesis is one
of these moments. Where evangelization is concerned with the
first proclamation of the Gospel made manifest in word and
deed and with initial conversion, catechesis moves beyond this
and is concerned with the teaching of the Christian message
"with a view to initiating the hearers into the fullness of Christian life" (*CT* 18).

Two other documents that need mention are the *Apostolic
Exhortation on the Vocation and the Mission of the Lay Faithful in
the Church and in the World (Christifideles Laici)* and *On the
Church's Missionary Mandate (Redemptoris Missio)*. Published
in 1988 and 1991 respectively, these documents serve as source
for an understanding of "new evangelization." In these documents we find the recognition of the various settings within
which evangelization takes place, the various audiences toward
whom evangelization is directed. The first setting is the classic
"mission *ad gentes*," that is the work with those who have not
known the Gospel. The second set of situations is those fundamentally Christian contexts where the need for continuing
evangelization is particularly important in addressing children
and youth. The final setting is found in Christian contexts where
the link between the Gospel and life is not evident or effective.
Here the focus of attention is "the baptized of all ages who live
in a religious context in which Christian points of reference are
perceived purely exteriorly" (*RM* 58). In this context there is a
need for a "new evangelization" or re-evangelization: the re-

newed proclamation of the heart of the Gospel that it might touch the hearts and lives of the hearers and contribute to the "formation of mature ecclesial communities" (*ChL* 34).

The themes that are present in these documents resonate throughout the *General Directory for Catechesis*.[13] Influenced by the perspective reflected in *Evangelii Nuntiandi* and echoed in *Redemptoris Missio*, the writers of the *Directory* ground the work of evangelization in the mission of Jesus Christ: it is Jesus as first evangelizer, proclaiming the reign of God "as the urgent and definitive intervention of God in history" (34), that the Church follows in its own evangelical mission. The *Directory* makes clear that evangelization is rooted in the very being of the Church, the Church existing in order to evangelize, in order to proclaim God's reign. Evangelization invites all to recognize the implications of lived Christian life for their own time and place: to hear the proclamation of the Gospel, to enter into the Christian life through the sacraments of Christian initiation, to be nourished by the community in living the Christian life, and to recognize and accept the responsibility to participate in the mission of the Church (see *GDC* 47–49). As such, evangelization as an ecclesial activity is not simply a series of activities or programs; it is not something to put on the parish's list of committees and activities. At its heart, evangelization has to do with *how the parish lives and makes all of its decisions.*

Returning to the idea that developed across these documents and is reflected in the *Directory*—that evangelization is as much about who we are as what we do—it might be helpful to think not only of the noun *evangelization* but of the descriptive form, *evangelizing*. When we use the term *evangelization*, there is the temptation to set it out as another activity the parish does—catechesis, liturgy, pastoral care, and evangelization. Or to see it as the responsibility of a single committee—the evangelization committee, similar to the other committees a parish might have, such as the social committee, the school committee, or the finance committee.

Using the word *evangelizing* strengthens the commitment that who we are as Church—our mission and identity—is rooted in engaging in all activities through the lens of evangelization. To speak of "evangelizing pastoral care," for example, reminds us that as we visit the sick, as we care for the bereaved or lonely, as we counsel the lost or confused, we do all of these activities in a way that recognizes the close connection between human life and the liberating word of Jesus Christ. We do all of these activities so as to proclaim the Gospel in word and action and thus further the reign of God. And so we can speak of evangelizing youth ministry, evangelizing liturgy, and even the evangelizing finance committee. And it is in this sense that we speak of evangelizing catechesis.

It is the reaffirmation of the church's mission to be and continue to become an evangelizing church that gives foundation to the call for ongoing catechesis of adults. It seems to me that this is one of the important contributions of the *GDC* to our understanding of adult catechesis. While church documents and catechetical leaders have been calling for adult faith formation for decades, it is the link between evangelization and catechesis that provides the clearest mandate and the most convincing rationale for focusing on adults. Adults need to be continually formed in their faith so that they are able to fulfill their responsibility in the mission of the church. The document *Adult Catechesis in the Christian Community* articulates this connection clearly:

> In summary, in order for the Good News of the Kingdom to penetrate all the various layers of the human family, it is crucial that every Christian play an active part in the coming of the Kingdom. . . . All of this naturally requires adults to play a primary role. Hence it is not only legitimate, but also necessary to acknowledge that a fully Christian community can only exist when a systematic catechesis of all its members takes place, and when an effective and well-developed catechesis of adults is regarded as the central task in the catechetical enterprise.[14]

This statement also makes clear the depth of the relationship between evangelization and catechesis. It is more than simply seeing evangelization as the invitation to first conversion and catechesis as the ongoing formation once that conversion has taken place. The relationship between evangelization and catechesis is more dynamic than that—evangelization sets the foundation for catechesis *and* catechesis is in service to the formation of an evangelizing community. The significant connection between evangelization and catechesis is that catechesis is in the service of the formation of an evangelizing people: a people who have as their focus living and proclaiming the Good News of the reign of God in order that it penetrate all the various layers of the human family. Catechesis must prepare them for this task!

Entering the Conversation

One of the central themes running through this book and my own convictions about adult faith formation and becoming an adult church is the centrality and necessity of sustained adult conversation. In many ways this book is an expression of my ongoing conversation with practitioners and theorists in religious education as well as theologians, educational theorists, and people involved in the social sciences. It is from those conversations that my sense of what it would mean to engage in catechesis toward an adult church has emerged.

Reading a text is also an invitation to conversation. We approach any text on a variety of levels. On one level we follow the narrative of the text, asking questions about the explicit events or images being presented or the ideas being explored. On a second level we are attempting to enter into the world being set out in the text. Here the focus is not simply on attending to the words of the text, but also understanding the "world" of the text; the world that allows the ideas being presented to have meaning and to be meaningful. A third level involves our entering into the text from our own world—the world of the reader. Our own experiences and perceptions of those experiences shape the way we read and interpret a text. We approach the text with our own pre-understanding, which provides the basis for our understanding of the text.[15] Our own pre-understandings both make possible and limit our understanding and engagement with the text.

An example might be helpful. The statement "The mission of the church is to evangelize" serves as a central theme for this chapter and for our understanding of adult faith formation. Without some understanding of the term *evangelization*, or to *evangelize*, the statement would not make any sense at all; the reader would be no closer to understanding the mission of the church. So, the reader's pre-understanding of the term makes possible any interpretation of the text. At the same time, if the reader has a narrow understanding of evangelization (i.e., equating it with proselytizing) his or her grasp of the statement and the implications the statement has for the nature of the church and adult faith formation is limited.

It is only by acknowledging and entering into the process by which my world shapes my engagement with the text and the text in turn shapes my world that I can authentically say that I *know* the text; it is here that genuine conversation with the text takes place. And in this process my pre-understandings are challenged, nuanced, clarified, corrected, affirmed, and so on. It is in the conversation between the world of the text and the world of the reader that learning takes place.

To assist this process, it is helpful to keep in mind a series of questions while reading the text: What section of the text do you find unclear? Why is it unclear? With what in the text do you strongly agree? Why? With what in the text do you strongly disagree? What is the basis of the disagreement? If you had the opportunity for dialog with the author, what would you want to say or ask about the aspect with which you disagree? As you read, what experiences or perceptions from your own life come to mind? How are these challenged and/or affirmed by the text?

In addition to one's conversation with the text, entering into sustained conversation with others who share a common interest and commitment to forming an adult church is rewarding and can be sustaining of one's passion and undertakings. At the end of each chapter, I include some questions as guides for your reflection and as possible starting points for conversation with others. The effectiveness of a book of this nature is not in its ability to provide clear answers but in its ability to help the reader articulate and explore clear questions.

FOR YOUR
REFLECTION AND CONVERSATION

1. What do you see as the central strengths to the way in which catechesis is understood in parishes today? What are some of the indicators that you recognize as signs of a need for shifting the focus of the prime question for catechesis?

2. "Catechesis is always in service to an ecclesiology. Whether that ecclesiology is articulated or not, whether the link is intentionally examined or not, our approach to catechesis and our understanding of its goals point to presumptions about the nature of the church." What presumptions about the nature and mission of the church do you see reflected in your understanding of catechesis?

3. "At a fundamental level, catechesis is not only in service to membership within a particular expression of Christianity, it is also in service to discipleship, the ability to live, to make decisions, in light of the Gospel and the reign of God." What is your reaction to this statement? In what ways does it confirm or challenge your understanding of the goal of catechesis?

4. What are the one or two key insights from this chapter that you will want to carry with you into the next sections of the text?

NOTES

1. Westerhoff writes: "While admitting that learning takes place in many ways, church education has functionally equated the context of education with schooling and the means of education with formal instruction. The public schools have provided us with our model of education, and insights from secular pedagogy and psychology have been our guides. A church school with teachers, subject matter, curriculum, resources, supplies, equipment, age-graded classes and classrooms, and, where possible, a professional church educator as administrator, has been the norm." John H. Westerhoff, *Will Our Children Have Faith?* (New York: Seabury Press, 1976), 9.

2. Westerhoff's major works in defining the foundations of catechesis include *Values for Tomorrow's Children: An Alternative Future for Education in the Church* (Philadelphia: Pilgrim Press, 1970); *Tomorrow's Church: A Community of Change* (Waco, TX: Word Books, 1976); *Inner Growth, Outer Change: An Educational Guide to Church Renewal* (New York: Seabury Press, 1979) and, with William H. Willimon, *Liturgy and Learning Through the Life Cycle* (New York: Seabury Press, 1980).

3. In an article titled "A Critical Definition of Adult Education" Stephen Brookfield points to six characteristics of adult education including voluntary participation, learner directed, and intended for transformation. While some of the characteristics which he includes may also be appropriate to the education of children and youth, the particular relationship of the constellation of characteristics is distinctively adult. *Adult Education Quarterly* 36 (Fall 1985): 44–49.

4. Many of the key catechetical documents published prior to 1995 have been collected into a single volume: Martin Connell, ed., *The Catechetical Documents: A Parish Resource* (Chicago: Liturgy Training Publications, 1996). For a discussion of the general development of the understanding of catechesis across these documents, see Jane Regan, "Principles of Catechesis from Ecclesial Documents," in *Empowering Catechetical Leaders*, eds. Thomas Groome and Michael Corso (Washington, DC: United States Catholic Conference, 1999).

5. Congregation for the Clergy, *General Directory for Catechesis (GDC)* (Washington DC: United States Catholic Conference, 1997). NCCB, *Our Hearts Were Burning Within Us, A Pastoral Plan for Adult Faith Formation in the United States (OHWB)*, (Washington, DC: United States Catholic Conference, 1999).

6. This is discussed at length in Chapter 5, where the implications of situating catechesis within the context of evangelization are explored.

7. Thomas Groome, "The Purpose of Christian Catechesis," in *Empowering Catechetical Leaders*, eds. Thomas Groome and Michael Corso (Washington, DC: National Catholic Educational Association, 1999).

8. Maria Harris in *Fashion Me a People* gives voice to the significance of the null curriculum within a community of faith and its role in forming the perspective and understandings of the members. Maria Harris, *Fashion Me a People: Curriculum in the Church* (Louisville, KY: Westminster/John Knox, 1989), 69.

9. This is discussed in detail in Chapter 3 where the insights of transformative learning as set out in adult education theory and practice are examined.

10. Congregation for the Clergy, *General Catechetical Directory* (1971). Reprinted in Martin Connell, ed., *The Catechetical Documents: A Parish Resource.*

11. Pope Paul VI, *On Evangelization in the Modern World (Evangelii Nuntiandi)* (1975), 18. Reprinted in Connell, ed., *The Catechetical Documents: A Parish Resource.*

12. Austin Flannery, ed. *Vatican Council II: Constitutions, Decrees, and Declarations.* Revised translation in inclusive language. (Northport, NY: Costello Publishing, 1996.) All quotes from the documents of Vatican II are from this edition. References are given in the text by paragraph number.

13. Congregation for the Clergy, *General Directory for Catechesis (GDC)* (Washington, DC: United States Catholic Conference, 1997). These documents were not written in a vacuum, so another way to explore the context for this discussion of the relationship between evangelization and catechesis is to look at the shifts and changes in the theory and practice of catechesis over the past fifty years or so. See Catherine Dooley, "Evangelization and Catechesis: Partners in the New Millennium" in *The Echo Within: Emerging Issues in Religious Education,* Catherine Dooley and Mary Collins, eds. (Allen, TX: Thomas More, 1997) 145–60. In that essay Dooley traces the convergence of issues from the liturgical movement, from the catechetical movement, and from a renewed understanding of mission and evangelization.

14. International Council for Catechesis, *Adult Catechesis in the Christian Community: Some Principles and Guidelines, with Discussion Guide* (Washington, DC: United States Catholic Conference, 1992), #25. Also available in Martin Connell, ed., *The Catechetical Documents: A Parish Resource.*

15. Here I am working out of the framework presented by Hans-Georg Gadamer and his understanding of hermeneutics. Rejecting an Enlightenment notion that it is preferred and possible in the reading of a text to ascertain the original meaning of the author, Gadamer argues that our engagement with a text is similar to a conversation. We bring into the reading our situation, our effective history, our prejudices or pre-understandings. The best reader/conversationalist is the one who can recognize those pre-understandings, and be willing to put them at risk and in service to genuine conversation. See Hans-Georg Gadamer, *Truth and Method,* 2d rev. ed. (New York: Continuum, 1999), particularly Chapter 11, "Elements of a Theory of Hermeneutical Experience."

2

THE ADULT AS
PERSON OF FAITH

O n a typical Sunday morning in an average Catholic parish in an urban, suburban, or rural area, who are the adults present? How do we describe the adult community? From one perspective this is a sociological question; and research conducted over the past decade provides some insight into the nature of the parish community as group. As we think about the formation of adults within the faith community, the question is not only about trends regarding beliefs and practices. From another angle provided by the intersection of psychology and theology, this is a question about the reality of being an adult within the contemporary Church and culture. So we look in on this typical Sunday morning not only for who is present (and who is absent) but for what might be their reflections or concerns as they enter the church building to become an assembly of God's people.

There is an assortment of families with two parents and two or three children; perhaps one of the parents is thinking about things at work while the other is wondering how well the youngest child is doing in school. In another family perhaps one of the parents has lost a satisfying and well-paying job; both adults in that family are wondering and worrying about money and bills and possible relocation. Another family—a professional couple with two children, perhaps—have just put earnest money down on a new dream home. They are startled to realize that the mortgage on the house is more than any one of their parents made in a lifetime, and they feel just a bit awkward, a little uncomfortable about that. And perhaps across from them is an elderly couple whose children are grown and established elsewhere; he remembers past liturgies when their family was young and the children were bracketed between them in the pew, and she looks to the future with a mix of contentment for a life well lived and some concern that they be able to maintain their independence.

There are some young couples in the assembly. Perhaps there is a twenty-something couple with fairly loose connections to the parish who have just given birth to their first child and are now looking to have their child baptized and also looking for something more that they cannot name. Perhaps there is a couple in their thirties who have always envisioned the future shaped by children and family life who now discover that they are unable to conceive without significantly invasive procedures that guarantee nothing.

There are a number of single people in the gathering. Perhaps for one a divorce came through this week; for another this might be the anniversary of a spouse's death recalled with poignancy over many years. A recent college graduate who is teaching in the local elementary school might be in the assembly. He is discovering that he really doesn't like teaching; the image of himself as an established and successful career teacher is fading, and he isn't sure what image might replace it. The single parents in the assembly think about money or how to juggle schedules, or they simply reflect on how nice it is to sit quietly for a few minutes in the midst of a hectic life.

While this is presented as a cross section of the reflections and concerns of those present on a Sunday morning, these same themes are pressing on those who are not present.[1] Perhaps they are thinking similar thoughts as they read the Sunday paper, head off for work, or return home from the gym. In each of these vignettes, core realities of adult experience and adult faith are disclosed. At some level, each of the people described is engaged in the process of *meaning making* which is at the heart of being human.

MEANING MAKING AS ADULTS

Meaning making refers to the fundamental activity of human being. To be human is to engage in the process of finding the patterns and forms and relationships that give unity and significance to one's life. It is the process of seeking coherency and meaningfulness in the elements of human existence. Every act of perception is an act of meaning making; it is a composing of reality.

For example, we see a collection of patterns and colors and shadings and recognize the elements that together define it as a bush: the leaves and stems, the intricacies of branches rising up from a common base. We make meaning from the collection of patterns and colors and shadings that we as active subjects take in through our senses. We may be able to go further and recognize it as a particular kind of bush. The shape and pattern of leaves, the color of the bark, and the shape of the base all come together in the meaning-making process and we recognize this as a lilac bush. Our past history and experience, the mood of the day, and our memory of other lilac bushes shape this process of meaning making. Each of us sees the same lilac bush and yet composes it, making meaning of it in different ways.

If we step back to look at the theorists within the social sciences who examine human development, the heart of what they explore is the way in which humans make meaning of their experience.[2] An important starting point for this look at human development is the writings of Jean Piaget with his concern for how human beings—particularly children—come to "know" the world around them.[3] Bringing together his interests as a philosopher and biologist, Piaget, as a genetic epistemologist, studied the nascent way of knowing that the infant uses to make meaning of sense perceptions and the development of that epistemology throughout childhood. His careful observation of children's ways of making meaning of the world has given us a schema for understanding children's reasoning, an invariant sequence of stages that children pass through as their structure of thinking becomes increasingly sophisticated. Each stage is reflective of a psychological structure that serves to organize and give order to one's engagement with the environment. For the developing child, each stage builds on the prior ones and represents a more sophisticated, complex, inclusive, and adequate way of viewing the world.

Age	Stage	Description
Infancy (0–1½ years)	Sensorimotor stage	characterized by a process of differentiating self from world and establishing basic temporal and spatial relationships
Early childhood (2–6 years)	Preoperational stage	defined by the acquisition of language and an understanding of the world based on one's own perceptions and intuition
Childhood (7–12 years)	Concrete operational stage	typified by the ability to apply concrete "operations" on the objects of knowing and with this an ability to distinguish the real from the imaginary
Adolescence (13+ years)	Formal operational stage	described as the ability to think about thinking; operations applied to concrete objects in the prior stage are now applied to the process of knowing

The foundational framework of Piaget is that the way in which we "know" the world has an impact on our reality. For the infant who lacks the concept of object permanence, the object taken away and placed under a blanket is not simply hidden and too hard to find—it does not exist. The development over the first two years is a development in the relationship between baby and object: the object comes to exist independent of the toddler's view or awareness of it. This is a process of differentiation between world and infant so that the object comes into being independent of the infant's sensing. The infant is embedded in his senses (the sensorimotor stage) and the world is created through that embeddedness. Moving up a stage, the five-year-old preoperational thinker is embedded in her perceptions. Placing the two cups side by side she calls "Unfair!" because the juice comes up higher in her sister's glass than in hers. No amount of reasoning with a five year old is going to convince her that the amount of juice in her short, fat cup is the same as the amount of juice in her sister's taller, more slender glass. Reality is created by the cognitive structures through which we interpret the world.

Central to Piaget's framework is the force, or activity, that moves development: the seeking of equilibrium.[4] Rooted as he is in biological constructs, he portrays the process of an organism's maintaining equilibrium within an environment as the dynamic process of accommodation and assimilation. This is at the core of his model for exploring the developing child's dynamic interaction with the world. Piaget argues that all organisms seek balance with their environment and that human activity can be understood as a continuous process of "readjustment or equilibration."[5]

Piaget describes the process of adaptation (assimilation and accommodation) as the move "first of all to incorporate things and people into the subject's own activity, i.e. to 'assimilate' the external world into the structures that have already been constructed, and secondly to readjust these structures as a function of subtle transformation, i.e., to 'accommodate' them to external objects."[6] Assimilation is the action of the subject on the object. Accommodation is the impact of the object on the subject and the subject's cognitive structures. The stages of cognitive development that Piaget names serve as points of relatively stable equilibration[7] when the ongoing dynamic interaction with the world (meaning making) takes place within the already existing structures.

A slight aside here, pointing in the direction of the significance of this for how we understand adult faith: our discussion of accommodation and assimilation is not applicable only to developing children whose cognitive growth is driven by the assimilation-accommodation pattern as they meaningfully interact with their environment. As adults we too are always engaged in forms of assimilation and accommodation. The mundane—though enjoyable—reading of a murder mystery is an example. Early on we create a theory of the resolution of the mystery. If we have read the author before, we have a good deal of data for how the mystery may end. The descriptions of characters, the positing of motives are assimilated into our theory as we move through the book's pages. But this information can also reshape the theory we have; it can lead to the accommodation of our theory so that it accounts for unsubstantiated alibis and misplaced murder weapons. Our point of equilibration—and the satisfactory solving of the mystery—is found in the complementary process of assimilation and accommodation. In situations more complex and life-defining than reading a murder mystery, our process of meaning making is essentially grounded in the process of equilibration.

While Piaget did not push his research beyond early adolescence, his contribution to our understanding of human cognition and reasoning cannot be overestimated. He established a developmental paradigm around human meaning making and established the dynamics of equilibration as describing the movement at the core of human maturing.

Piaget's research became the foundation for a number of developmental theories that looked at various dimensions of human becoming. Theories such as those of Lawrence Kohlberg[8] (moral development), Carol Gilligan[9] (moral development among women), Robert Selman[10] (role taking), William Perry[11] (intellectual and ethical development of college students), and James Fowler[12] (faith development) have their foundations in the dynamics of the paradigm set out by Piaget. Each of the theories—referred to as structural developmental theories or constructivist theories—examines some dimension of the way in which human beings "develop" and actively make meaning of the world around them. These theories posit a sequential, hierarchical, generally invariant schema through which the person passes in his or her development.

We will return to this foundational framework with a careful look at the contribution that James Fowler has made to the understanding of faith and the stages of faith development. But Piaget's theory and those of the neo-Piagetian theorists who followed him do not tell the entire story of human beings' engagement and meaning making in the world.[13] Complementing Piaget's theory of cognitive development—the cognitive constructivist approach to human meaning making—is the work of scholars examining human activity from the perspective of the psychological and social context within which it takes place. Here the research of Erik Erikson is particularly useful.[14]

Like Piaget's, Erikson's theory serves as the foundation for other theorists who have explored and expanded his framework. Like Piaget, Erikson is interested in the individual-world relationship and how the person makes sense of the experience of the world. Like Piaget, Erikson is setting out a series of stable points that individuals pass through as they move through their lives. But Erikson's lens is different: he is looking at the matrix— the psychological and social context—that shapes the individual's ability to engage effectively with his or her experience of the world. His theory serves as the foundation of the psychosocial developmental theories.[15]

Central to Erikson's schema is the construct of "life cycle." Imaged as a spiral (rather than the steps and levels that one would connect with Piaget), the life cycle conveys the sense that the individual life gathers together into a coherent whole and that themes and issues that are considered at one point reappear in other forms and from other perspectives later in life. Erikson conveys this by speaking of the life cycle as an "epigenetic cycle." Drawing on the model set out by embryologists, Erikson argues that major life issues have a period in which they come to ascendancy, but they are present at other times as well. The clearest example is the issue that comes to the fore during adolescence: one's ability to maintain a sense of internal sameness across the variety of experiences. At this point in the life cycle, the adolescent is attempting to address the tension ("crisis") experienced between identity formation and identity diffusion. But that crisis is anticipated in the earlier points in the individual's life—in the sharp "No!" of the two year old, for example—and renegotiated in later ones—in the reflections of the elderly on the meaningfulness of their lives.[16]

Stage	Crisis	Virtue
Infancy	Basic trust vs. Basic mistrust	Hope
Early childhood	Autonomy vs. Shame, doubt	Will
Play age	Initiative vs. Guilt	Purpose
School age	Industry vs. Inferiority	Competence
Adolescence	Identity vs. Identity confusion	Fidelity
Young adulthood	Intimacy vs. Isolation	Love
Adulthood	Generativity vs. Stagnation	Care
Old age	Integrity vs. Despair	Wisdom

For Erikson, the person's life cycle is defined by crises, or turning points. Brought on by the person's developing physical, intellectual, psychological, and social worlds, these crises are necessary and unavoidable points in life "when development must move one way or another, marshaling resources of growth, recovery and further differentiation."[17] Described in terms of tension between two states or ways of perceiving one's self in the world—between trust and mistrust, between autonomy and shame or doubt, between initiative and guilt, and so forth—the successful negotiation of each stage is to establish a healthful ratio of the first variable over the second, the syntonic over the dystonic. We want the school-aged child to have a healthful view of her participation in the work of her group and society (industry). This is balanced by the experience of inferiority, the concern that the tools and skills that she has are not as good as others and are not adequate to the work. Establishing a healthful resolution, or truce, between the variables of each period produces the strength, or virtue, corresponding to the need of each age. For a seven or eight year old whose industry prevails over inferiority, the strength is a sense of competence.

Linked as it is to predictable social, intellectual, and psychological developments, Erikson's schema provides us with a description of expected crises that will need to be negotiated at fairly predictable points in a person's life.[18] Whether negotiated well or poorly, the individual takes the resolution of each crisis and the strength (or lack of strength) that has eventuated into the next life period.

The resolution of the crisis has impact beyond the individual's life; Erikson's concern for the social and relational dimension of human meaning making is expressed in his attention to the intergenerational impact of the life cycle. Picture the spiral of the person's life cycle superimposed on the life cycle from the prior generation and serving as the foundation for that of the generation to follow. This series of intertwined spirals reminds us, for example, that the ability of a significant adult to negotiate the crisis of generativity vs. stagnation serves as a framework for the adolescent's growing sense of identity. And the way in which the adult negotiated the identity formation vs. identity diffusion some years back impinges on his or her ability to mentor the adolescent now.

DYNAMICS OF DEVELOPMENT

Piaget (and those within the same paradigm) and Erikson (and those who attend to the psychosocial context) present us angles of vision on the stages and cycles of the meaning making process of adults gathered in that Sunday morning assembly described at the opening of this chapter. Having a sense of the life "crisis" that frames a person's interpretive world, or of the tools that a person is using to make meaning of experience, is helpful. But the fascination with stages and levels and the potential for differentiating the frameworks for the interpreted experience of a gathered group of adults can at times block the view of the common dynamics of movement that propel human growth and development. While the theories mentioned thus far differ in focus, it is possible and helpful to recognize some commonality in these theories by giving consideration to the force for change and development that rests behind them. And I would argue that in considering the dynamic catalyst of human development we can most easily find the reality of what it means to be a person of faith, to be a person of *adult faith.*

One entry point for considering the question of the relationship between human development and religious or spiritual growth is the work of Robert Kegan. He proposes that changing the parameters of what we look at as we examine the dynamics of human development can more easily open up this question.[19] Although recognizing the significance and contribution of the structural-developmental school,[20] Kegan argues that "With very few exceptions, the work of Piagetians ('neo' or oth-

erwise) must still be characterized as about *cognition*, to the neglect of *emotion*; the *individual*, to the neglect of the *social*; the
epistemological, to the neglect of the *ontological* (or *concept*, to
the neglect of *being*); *stages* of meaning constitution, to the neglect of meaning-constitution *process* and (forgive the awkward
expression of this last) what is *new and changed* about a person,
to the neglect of *the person who persists through time*."[21] Whether
one could or would want to refute parts of this statement,
Kegan's point is worth noting: all of the "neglects" are connected
with a tendency within these theories to limit attention to the
stages themselves. Kegan argues that behind these multiple neglects is a fundamental disregard of the essential context within
which to set a stage theory; Kegan refers to this as "meaning-
constitutive-evolutionary activity."[22]

To break open the meaning of adult development and to
disclose the religious or spiritual dimension of human existence
and human growth is to look beyond the foreground of stages
to the background of the motion of human be-ing. Kegan
writes, "Put more simply, I am saying that persons are not their
stages of development; persons are a motion, a creative motion,
the motion of life itself."[23] Kegan points out that the stages are
simply markers that point to "periods of dynamic stability in
the motion that is the activity of human being."[24] Kegan's interest is to name the religious or spiritual dimension of human development inherent to its motion and stages, and in order to do
so he proposes looking at three key phenomena of this meaning-constitutive-evolutionary activity. "The first is the apparently universal tension between the longing to be included,
attached, 'a part of,' on the one hand, and the longing to be dis-
tinct, separate, autonomous on the other. The second is the apparently universal and recurring experience of losing and
recovering a sense of meaning and order. And the third is the
apparently universal need to be recognized."[25]

As Kegan examines the meaning of these three phenomena,
it is clear that they are elements of a common process of main-

taining balance or equilibration in knowing of self and world. Each developmental era represents a balance in the way the person negotiates the three dimensions of meaning-constitutive-evolutionary activity. Each stage represents a particular way of negotiating the relationship "between the move toward differentiation and the move toward integration,"[26] as well as between one's present evolutionary truce (how the person knows the world now) and the future construction. And with each developmental era comes the need to be recognized within the process of development.[27]

For Kegan, this dynamic of maintaining balance and engaging disequilibrium as an indicator of the partial nature of our present evolutionary truce has the potential of pointing to the religious dimension of life. Facing into the inadequacy of our present balance—our present meaning making—the "More" (not Kegan's vocabulary) is revealed. Kegan writes: "H. Richard Niebuhr and Paul Tillich both help us move from this empirical reality to the religious in their understanding of the tension between the preliminary (the present construction of self and others) and the ultimate (the ground of being in which this construction lives)."[28] To repeat: our awareness of the partiality of our present constitution of self and world—a partiality made clear with the experience of loss of meaning, of the end of the present evolutionary truce, of dis-equilibration—serves as a hint of the "More" of the "ground of being."

David Tracy points to a similar dynamic when he writes of the role of "limit-experiences," those times when we are confronted by the "limit-to" our human existence. These experiences—"finitude, contingency, mortality, alienation or oppression"[29]—disclose the corresponding "limit-of" our human being, point to the reality of the transcendent dimension, the "more" of human existence. These experiences make possible the recognition of the partiality of our present construction of reality.[30] At our best we recognize that all of our constructions of self and world—present as well as future—are only partial; more often, having weathered the move through loss of meaning to a new construction of self and others, we imagine we have arrived. But reminded again by experiencing the limit-to our human existence, we have the potential of recognizing that limit experience as revelatory.

FAITH AND MEANING MAKING

The themes we have considered thus far serve as helpful foundations for our understanding of the way faith develops and of the referent for the words "adult faith." Three concepts can serve us in our understanding of faith development: that the activity of human be-ing is essentially a meaning-making activity; that the movement of human development is impelled forward in the essential work of continually reestablishing equilibrium in the dynamic relationship of knowing self and world; and that this process of embracing the loss of meaning or disequilibrium in order to make way for a new meaning has the potential to be revelatory of the "More."

One of the most influential researchers shaping the way we speak about faith and faith development is James Fowler. His writings of more than twenty years provide important insights into the nature of developing faith as well as the role of adult faith in the public Church. Attempting to keep a theoretical foot in the psychosocial perspective of Erikson as well as in the structural development school of Piaget and those who followed his framing of the developmental question,[31] Fowler proposes a model for understanding the sequential movement of the person's faith-knowing. He proposes sequential, hierarchical, and invariable stages that a person may pass through beginning in infancy and continuing to old age—each stage representing a more sophisticated, complex, and inclusive way of "faithing" in the world. As with other developmental theorists, Fowler proposes that the movement from one stage to the next is the active meaning-making subject's response to his or her engagement with the sociocultural world. Shifting intellectual, psychological, and social worlds viewed in one stage provide the required, though not necessarily sufficient, conditions for movement to subsequent stages.

To draw out the implications of Fowler's schema of faith development in ways helpful to this conversation on adult faith, we begin with the definition, or description, of faith that grounds Fowler's theory. A brief introduction of the early stages sets the context for considering the adult stages of faith and the dynamics that facilitate movement from one stage to the next. We conclude this chapter by articulating implications of developmental theories for the process of fostering adult faith, movement toward an adult church.

Defining Faith

Working out of the tradition of Paul Tillich and Richard Niebuhr, Fowler understands faith as a universal human concern. In *Stages of Faith* he expresses the fundamental role of faith within the quintessential human activity: meaning making. "Faith is a person's or group's way of moving into the force field of life. It is our way of finding coherence in and giving meaning to the multiple forces and relations that make up our lives. Faith is a person's way of seeing him- or herself in relation to others against a background of shared meaning and purpose."[32] Faith has "to do with the making, maintenance and transformation of human meaning."[33] Used in this sense, faith differs from belief. Belief refers to the categorical expression of that toward which the individual expresses or experiences faith. "Belief, in religious contexts, at least, arises out of the effort to translate experiences of and relations to transcendence into concepts or propositions."[34] Faith refers to the basic orientation of the person, the way in which he or she knows the world and engages in the activity of meaning making. As such, faith is not necessarily theistic or even religious. The "object" of one's faith—the ultimate environment in which the centers of value have mean-

ing and unity—provides the context for the constitutive meaning-making activity. An explication of Fowler's definition sheds
light on this:

> The process of constitutive knowing
> Underlying a person's composition and maintenance of a
>   comprehensive frame (or frames) of meaning
> Generated from the person's attachment or commitment to
>   centers of supraordinate value which have the power to
>   unify his or her experiences of the world
> Thereby endowing the relationships, contexts and patterns
>   of everyday life, past and future with significance.[35]

Two core elements of faith reflected in this definition are
particularly important for our understanding of adult faith.
First, faith is "the process of constitutive knowing." That is, in
the process of knowing the world, the subject is "known" as well.
The constructive knowing of Piaget makes clear that we con-
struct/establish/make meaning of the world around us through
the application of structures and operations. To say that faith is
constitutive knowing is to say that it is a self-constituting activity: the self is also being shaped by the way in which the self sees
the world. "In these kinds of constitutive-knowing not only is
the 'known' being constructed but there is also a simultaneous
confirmation, modification, or reconstitution of the *knower in
relation to the known*."[36] This is a knowing that extends beyond
the bounds of reason in the sense that Piaget uses it. The major
concern for Piaget is how children reason about the world, how
they know and construct the world. From Fowler's perspective,
this is rooted in a "logic of rational certainty." The move into
the constitutive knowing of faith necessitates setting this "logic
of rational certainty" within the more comprehensive way of
knowing based on a "logic of conviction."[37] In the act of knowing or meaning making that is faith knowing, the self is at risk as
well; the self is "under construction," or being remolded, along
with the world.

We recognize this type of knowing when we are trying to reach a life-defining decision. The application of "logic of rational certainty" results in a helpful clarification of a situation and the range or possible resolutions. But in the final analysis, when asked why one option was chosen over another, our response is often, "I can't explain it; I just *knew* that was the right thing to do." This kind of knowing is rooted in our values and convictions as well as in our understanding of that which gives ultimate meaning to our lives: our "center of supraordinate value."

Central to Fowler's notion of faith is the dynamic of relationship, the second element of his description of faith that merits further attention. The foundation of all human faith is relationship.[38] The first major task in Erikson's framework of development is negotiating the relationship between trust and mistrust worked out in a relationship of mutuality with the primary caregiver. As the child develops a sense of the reliability of the care of the parent, a sense of the trustworthiness of the world and of his or her place in the world becomes secure. This trust, commitment, attachment to the parent serves as the foundation for all later relationships and for the person's ability to commit to anyone or anything.[39]

While this interpersonal relationship of trust is essential, Fowler examines the relational characteristics of faith by looking at its fundamentally triadic structure. What makes the relationship between people or within a community viable is not simply the strength of the relationship between two (or more) persons but the shared trust in a common set of values and point of reference. Fowler writes: "But our ties to others are mediated, formed and deepened by our shared or common trust in and loyalties to centers of supraordinate value."[40] These triadic relationships of faith serve as the foundation for interpreting the world and our everyday experiences.

We are always engaged in multiple relationships of faith and trust with a variety of centers of supraordinate value. I am a parent in a specific triadic relationship with my daughters; we share together common values around family and relationships. I am a member of a university faculty and those within the university share a common commitment to academic freedom, intellectual integrity, and the centrality of the act of inquiry. I am a member of a parish, a town, a state, and a nation: in each of these cases those relations are defined and strengthened by our common commitment to shared centers of supraordinate value. What gives meaning and unity to these multiple triads? Here we draw on Fowler's notion of "ultimate environment," which refers to the widest arena within which the person makes meaning of his or her life. It is "a comprehensive frame of meaning that both holds and grows out of the most transcendent centers of value and power to which our faith gives allegiance."[41] "In Jewish and Christian terms, the ultimate environment is expressed with the symbol 'Kingdom of God.' In this way of seeing, *God* is the center of power and value which unifies and gives character to the ultimate environment."[42]

We speak of faith, then, as a constitutive knowing in which the active, meaning-making subject as well as the world is being constructed, shaped. We speak of faith in relational terms, relationships with centers of supraordinate value that are unified within the center, which is most inclusive and most comprehensive: the ultimate environment. It is the relationship with this center that, in the words of the description of faith given previously, underlies a person's "composition and maintenance of a comprehensive frame (or frames) of meaning . . . thereby endowing the relationships, contexts and patterns of everyday life, past and future, with significance."

Stages of Faith

With the framework of Fowler's understanding of faith, we turn now to look at his stages of faith,[43] with eventual focus on the adult stages. Keep in mind that we understand each stage of faith not as a single entity but as a unified syndrome of ways in which persons engage with the world and with their ultimate center of supraordinate value.

The first three stages of Fowler's schema—numbered 0 through 2—describe the faith perspective of childhood and correlate with the movement of intellectual development articulated by Piaget. The prestage (0) of undifferentiated faith establishes the foundation of trust and hope and the experience of mutuality that is essential for the later faith development. It is here that the prelanguage, prethought experiences that serve as the foundation for our earliest images of God are found.[44]

The transition into Stage 1 comes about with the introduction of thought and language and the move to the preoperational stage of cognitive development (Piaget). *Stage 1 Intuitive-Projective faith* is typical of children ages three to seven. Characterized by imaginative processes which "are unrestrained and uninhibited by logical thought,"[45] the child is very much influenced by the examples and stories of faith expressed by significant adults; it is the adults that add coherency and meaning to life. Transition for the child into the next stage is facilitated with the development of concrete operational thinking (Piaget) and with the beginning of a distinction between what is real and what only seems to be.

Beginning around the ages of six or seven and continuing until eleven or twelve, the child moves into *Stage 2 Mythic-Literal faith*. During this stage, the child takes on the stories, beliefs, and customs of the community that shape the ultimate environment into which the child is socialized. The stories and myths of the community are important, but they are seen primarily as separate vignettes; the framework of an overall story into which they fit is not yet in place. Fowler uses the image of a river: At this stage the child can stand in the river and tell the stories and something of the logic of the stories, but he or she cannot get on the bank of the river and see the context for the stories.[46]

The transition between Stages 2 and 3 is launched by the growing ability to think in the abstract, to think about thoughts.

The rise of formal operational thinking allows the child to begin to reflect upon the meaning of the stories inherited in the earlier stages. Recognition of clashes or contradictions in the stories received and a move away from literalism make such reflection necessary. There is also a growing recognition that others do not believe the way "we" do, and with this comes the need to enter into the story a bit more on one's own.

The characteristics that mark *Stage 3 Synthetic-Conventional faith* generally coalesce around the age of 12 or 13 and can serve as an adequate faith perspective into adulthood, and for many throughout life. As the title of the stage indicates, the focus here is on creating a system or structure within which the stories, images, and values can be worked together into a useable whole. This synthesis takes place and is defined in relationship to a group. While the reference group is larger than in the earlier stages—from parent, to family, to extensions of family—there is nonetheless a perspective of faith in which what "we" do and what "we" believe are important. This "we" can become increasingly sophisticated over time as the focal point of the defining convention moves from local parish to wider church. Within Stage 3 there is a growing ability to recognize what is central to one's reference group and what is not. The growing sophistication of conventional faith as it is expressed in adulthood is nonetheless shaped by what "we" believe and the values that "we" hold.

Adult Faith Stages

The movement from the prestage through Stage 3 is fundamentally the result of socialization. In Stage 3 the worldview that has formed and been formed by the person's primary reference groups is synthesized and internalized. The process of taking in (assimilation) and actively interpreting and making meaning (accommodation) of new experiences introduced through the developing child's and adolescent's intellectual capacity and his or her expanding social world takes place within the established frame of meaning of the dominant reference groups. The process of socialization leads to a coherent framework for meaning making and faith knowing that can sustain a person throughout life.

But what if the coherent framework comes under challenge by internal disagreement or contradiction? What happens when valued authority sources—the defining agents of what "we" believe—begin to disagree among themselves? What happens when the person's expanding world introduces him or her to people with differing beliefs and ways of life? when "they" are recognized as worthy of admiration and emulation? when "they" offer a viable and attractive alternative to what "we" believe? And what happens when the belief system or the image of God, which were received in this process of socialization, are inadequate for dealing with the challenges of life? These are all factors that initiate the transition into *Stage 4 Individuated-Reflective faith.*

Often taking place in the early twenties, though for many it does not emerge until mid-thirties or beyond, Stage 4 is, in effect, a leaving home, leaving the often tacitly held worldview that has been received and moving into one's own explicit worldview. With this comes a reinterpretation of one's self-identity; where previously it had been shaped as an amalgamation of the variety of roles one sustained in relationship within the significant reference groups, now one begins to define the self as identifiable beyond that context. For the established Stage 4 faith, I am first myself and then part of the group. "Self (identity) and outlook (worldview) are differentiated from those of others and become acknowledged factors in the reactions, interpretations and judgments one makes on the actions of the self and others."[47] With this comes "an interruption of reliance on external sources of authority."[48] While it is influenced by the views of others, the final arbiter of decision making is the internal conviction and personally appropriated values that form the individual's frame of meaning. Fowler makes the point that the elements of this double move—setting aside one's inherited worldview in favor of one that is reflectively appropriated *and* replacing external sources of authority with authority within one's self—do not always go together. This results in a "potentially longlasting equilibrium in a transitional position between Stages 3 and 4." [49]

An essential element of the move into Stage 4 is a "demythologizing" of the symbols, myths, and rituals of the tradition. It is a time of "more or less critical demythologization in which the import of a symbol, ritual or myth is separated from the entity itself and is conveyed in terms of ideas or propositions." [50] The emphasis on articulating a personally coherent, internally consistent framework of meaning leads the person living out of Stage 4 to value the symbolic as meaningful if it can be translated into propositions or conceptual formulations. The symbols have lost their power to serve as a point of entry into the transcendent. It is often this foundational "accomplishment" that serves as the platform for the transition into Stage 5. Fowler describes it this way: "Stories, symbols, myths and paradoxes from one's own or other traditions may insist on breaking in upon the neatness of the previous [Stage 4] faith. Disillusionment with one's compromises and recognition that life is more complex than Stage 4's logic of clear distinctions and abstract concepts can comprehend, press one toward a more dialectical and multileveled approach to life truth." [51]

Stage 5 Conjunctive faith is characterized by a postcritical reappropriation of the symbols of one's own tradition and of the power of symbols to be transformative of human consciousness. One is able to suspend one's critical skills and engage again in the symbols, myths, and rituals of one's tradition. [52] There is a reinterpretation and reintegration of the richness of aspects of faith from earlier stages and a willingness to live with the ambiguity that such a reintegration generates. At Stage 5, I am able again to be overwhelmed by the power of First Fire of

Easter while still being able, at a later time, to step
tique the liturgical event in light of ritual theory ar

Fowler describes the person at Stage 5 as enga
logical knowing. "In dialogical knowing the multipl
of the world is invited to disclose itself. In a mutual 'speaking'
and 'hearing,' knower and known converse in an I-Thou relationship. The knower seeks to accommodate her or his knowing to the structure of that which is being known before
imposing her or his own categories upon it."[53]

This renewed openness to one's own tradition, the ability to
engage and live with ambiguity, and the mode of dialogical
knowing contribute to one's perspective on truth. Where once
truth was defined within the confines of the "we" (Stage 3) or
circumscribed by the individual's personally appropriated
framework (Stage 4), the person at Stage 5 recognizes the multilayered reality to truth. This contributes to the apperception
that each articulation of truth is only partial and always in need
of being complemented by the insights of other traditions. As
Fowler points out, the relativity of the various traditions is not
only in relationship to one another but in their common relativity to that which they are attempting to mediate.[54]

As with the other stages, the seeds of the transition to *Stage
6 Universalizing faith* are found in the characteristics of Stage 5.
The genuine awareness and openness to the other and the appreciation of the symbols and myths of other traditions that are
part of Stage 5 serve as a prerequisite for the movement to Stage
6. While recognizing the possibility of an inclusive community,
a person embodying Stage 5 "lives and acts between an un-
transformed world and a transforming vision and loyalties."[55]
The person with Stage 6 faith works to give expression to the
most inclusive of ultimate environments both in his or her own
person and in the structures of society which oppress. The
movement into Stage 6 takes place in response to situations of
oppression and the "direct experience of the negation of one's

personhood or in one's identification with the negations experienced by others."[56] While reaching Stage 6 is rare, the impact of those people whom Fowler names as its representatives is significant: Martin Luther King, Jr., Dag Hammarskjöld, Gandhi.[57] Their significant contribution to the transformation of world without regard for the preservation of self is unquestionable. Fowler holds Stage 6 persons to "the criteria of inclusiveness of community, of radical commitment to justice and love and of selfless passion for a transformed world, a world made over not in *their* images, but in accordance with an intentionality both divine and transcendent."[58]

This overview of Fowler's stages of faith gives us a way to speak about adult, maturing faith. However, remember the insight that Kegan offers: the stages are effectively perceived as markers of relative equilibrium in a dynamic movement of meaning-constitutive-evolutionary activity. In light of that, while the charts that describe in short lines the shifts across stages of the various characteristics that define the nature of each stage might be helpful,[59] they belie the process of movement that is more fluid than those charts can indicate.

And yet, having some sense of the movement across the stages of the individual's locus of authority, bounds of social awareness, and understanding of symbols can be helpful. Perhaps a more disclosive way to speak of these movements is in story and images. With what can we compare the movement across Stages 3, 4, and 5? It is like the unfolding of a great dancer.

As a child she simply loved to dance; she was mesmerized by music and enchanted with movement. She was regularly surprised and delighted with what she could make her body do in dance. She'd rather dance than walk, and it often seemed that music was playing in her head and was expressed in the sway of her body and the tap of her toes as she was busy with work and play.

From a young age she took lessons; she was really very good and engaged in these lessons and recitals as yet another opportunity for dance. While in high school she was regularly a key part of the annual musicals. In addition to dancing herself, she worked with other students helping them to master the intricacies of the choreography. It was interesting though: even the least adept dancers were not put off or intimidated by her superior abilities; instead they felt supported and encouraged by her guidance, sharing in her enthusiasm for dance.

As she moved into adulthood she began to study the discipline of dance. She built her foundation on the forms and movements of classic dancers and studied the physiology of her body and used it to full advantage. She learned the structure of choreographed movements and the pressure of long hours of practice. She became an experienced and sought-after professional dancer: She was never out of place, she never missed a cue.

And yet something was missing: She was technically perfect but she came to realize that that was not enough. She was no longer mesmerized by movement, surprised by the grace of her own body. She was a good dancer, but found that she yearned for reclaiming the love of dance she had known as a child. Then, bringing the movements of dance, which were learned in the very fiber of her body from the years of discipline, into harmony with the passion for dance that she had known in her heart as a child, she became a great dancer.

The movement across these stages, from 3 to 4 to 5, represents both a movement out of expansion and a turning inward. Across these stages is a moving out from one's world; one's awareness of others and the ability to take the perspective of others is an enlarging movement. On the other hand, there is also a turning inward to claim an authority in one's own wisdom as it is read within the wisdom of the community. There is a returning to re-embrace the richness of symbols and myths that had shaped one's childhood faith. The genius of the dancer is that she moved out into the world of dance and back into her memory of dancing.

The overview of the stages of faith gives us some insights into the way in which dimensions of faith-knowing are constituted by the active subject. Each stage and transition marks a renegotiation of the meaning framework of the individual. It also serves as a reminder of the reality of the complexity of adult faith.

DEVELOPMENTAL THEORIES: SOME CAVEATS

Although Fowler's work is recognized by many as a helpful tool in understanding adult faith, too simplistic an application of it is problematic. Most people who critique developmental theories are not interested in totally dismissing the helpfulness of exploring the way in which a person's faith changes over time and the dynamics that effect that change. However, before proceeding to explore some of the implications of this discussion for adult faith formation and the movement toward an adult church, it is important to step back and raise some concerns about developmental theories in general and Fowler's theory of faith development in particular.

The first set of concerns has to do with developmental theories in general, particularly those based on the structural developmental perspective utilized by Piaget.[60] Most of these theories argue that the stages are sequential, hierarchical, and universal, and it is this claim that can be problematic.

While those who establish these theories affirm the adequacy of the lower stages, to speak of them as sequential and hierarchical leads to the conclusion that there is an evaluative element to being at a higher or lower stage—if the higher stages are more inclusive, more sophisticated, and so on. While in their origin—with Piaget, for example—the stages were seen simply as descriptive; the move into adult stages has tended to shift the structural developmental stage theory work from descriptive to prescriptive.

Fowler himself has recognized the difficulty of setting up a sequential, hierarchical stage theory without having it be seen as normative and prescriptive.[61] While arguing first that each stage is adequate and complete in itself, Fowler nonetheless sees Stage 6 as the normative endpoint. And Fowler is clearly arguing that his faith stages provide a guideline and direction for religious education. While arguing that each stage has an integrity of its own, Fowler nonetheless sees his theory as "a descriptive and normative model in relation to which the adequacy of our particular ways of being in faith can be assessed and faced."[62]

Here is the problem for the religious educator and for those who are imagining ways in which adults can grow in their faith: Is the goal to move people along the faith development stages?[63] Or to allow each person to live most authentically within her or his present stage? Or something in between? This touches at the very heart of the way in which we define the vision of adult faith formation. It also raises questions concerning the nature of the Church: can we and should we imagine a faith community where most of the members are Stage 5? Does the Church, in general, or a parish faith community, in particular, support the movement from the conforming nature of the person in Stage 3 to the distancing tendencies that are inevitable in the movement into and through Stage 4 to the embracing of the alternatives which is at the heart of someone living and "faithing" within Stage 5? Recognizing the complexity of that question is essential to the work of those engaged in adult catechesis. So, for the catechetical leader, the issue is to consider the question *behind* the framework of adult faith theory.

A second core issue that applies to developmental theories in general is one that was raised already in dialog with Kegan: What are we looking at when we speak of faith-stage development—the stage or the movement behind the stage? Kegan argues that most stage theories attend to the brief point of equilibrium that the stage serves to mark, rather than the "dance" that makes up the ebb and flow of human knowing and "faithing."[64] For Kegan the issue is not the stage but the movement generated (1) in the tension between being a part of something and being separate; (2) in the tension between losing and making meaning; and (3) in the need to be recognized within the process of development. For the catechetical leader I am convinced that this means attending with genuine care to the movements of faith—to the constitutive evolutionary activity to which Kegan points.

As we turn specifically to Fowler's faith-stage theory, other issues arise that warrant the attention of catechetical leaders. The first has to do with Fowler's separation of faith from content of faith—it is in this context that he would argue for the universality of his stages. Fowler is asserting that separating the dynamic of faith-knowing from the propositions of belief allows us to see the universally applicable movement of stages beneath the specific expression of faith. Fowler is arguing that however you define your "ultimate environment" (human achievement, democracy, socialism, capitalism, or the God of the Judeo-Christian tradition) the way in which these core "centers of supraordinate value" function and the way in which a person relates to them in making meaning of life is the same. Is that really possible or advisable?

One of the strongest critics of Fowler's claim to separate faith from belief is Gabriel Moran.[65] At the core of Moran's issue with Fowler is Moran's insistence that account must be taken of the role of language and particularly religious language to reveal. "Kingdom of God" and "Commonwealth of Love" cannot be used interchangeably as Fowler attempts to do.[66] This is true not just for Christians but for any who are attempting to name that which gives meaning to their lives. *God, love, kingdom, commonwealth*—all of those words have an effective history that prevents their being used interchangeably as referents for one's "ultimate environment." In the final analysis, there is a significance and importance in using the language of one's tradition to speak of the movement of faith.

An additional critique of Fowler's attempt to separate faith-knowing from belief looks to the question: What is he actually examining? Craig Dykstra serves as a good example of those who address this question. Dykstra believes that there is an essential value in defining faith from within a specific tradition and inviting others to do the same. For Dykstra, defined within the Christian tradition, faith is "appropriate and intentional participation in the redemptive activity of God."[67] Where in Fowler's understanding of faith, the construction of meaning is the goal, Dykstra argues that the outcome of faith and meaning is not constructed but appropriated in light of one's relationship with God.

For the catechetical minister, the implications for our understanding of faith and faith development are significant. Growth in faith, particularly up to late adolescence, is about developing an ever clearer sense of God's presence and action and what it means to participate in the redemptive act. Fowler's stages (like those of Piaget) might be helpful for understanding how children and young people attain and understand the sense of divine presence, but this is not faith. The fundamental sense of growth in faith is defined from within the tradition; it is within the faith tradition that the "appropriate and intentional participation in the redemptive activity of God" is defined. This is a theological task, Dykstra argues, rather than a social-scientific one. In the final analysis, Dykstra finds Fowler's research helpful, but contends that Fowler simply isn't talking about faith.

One final group of concerns is raised by those who question the methodology of the project. Maria Harris contends that it is problematic that all of the data is collected in verbal and discursive form: the research is dependent on analysis of interviews. Harris sees that this limits what we think faith is and how we express it.[68] It is telling that the first stage of Fowler's theory, which is prelanguage and continues until the child is eighteen months to two years, is understood as a *pre*stage, as though it does not really count in the discussion of faith development. And yet, from a variety of perspectives, this prestage is the most important, as it establishes the young child's sense of trust and of the faithfulness of the world. Without those, the other stages have little on which to build.

These are significant critiques of elements of Fowler's faith-stage theory, and they do need to be taken into account. How-ever, the contribution that Fowler has made to the way in which we understand the dynamics of growth in faith cannot be dis-missed. In light of our understanding of Fowler, we can engage more emphatically and effectively with the parent who is con-cerned because her daughter doesn't know the "basics." We can be more supportive of the young adult who seems to be "losing his faith" and recognize it as a necessary and important move in his faith development. And we can appreciate the fifty-some-thing woman who is finding that her commitment to our com-mon faith tradition is enhanced by her recognition of "truth" in the faith traditions of others. These are the insights that flow from Fowler's theory, and they are well worth treasuring.

FOSTERING ADULT FAITH

What can the ideas and insights examined in this chapter say to the understanding and process of adult faith formation? That question serves as a focus for this last section of the chapter. On a fundamental level, it gives some insight into the issues, rhythms, and complexities of adult lives and the dynamics at the heart of one's engagement with the tradition. In addition it gives some indication of the potential role of the community in sup-porting faith development and in supporting those who are ne-gotiating periods of loss of meaning.

Stepping back and examining the complexity of human de-velopment and its relationship with faith development provides a way for us to speak in general terms about the makeup and experience of the people gathered on a Sunday morning and en-gaged in a process of adult formation. While the lens each theorist picks up in looking at and describing the adult differs, the result is an image of complex active subjects engaged in the practice of constituting the reality of their lives. Theories within the psychosocial perspective provide us with some reading on the interpretive framework within which the individual makes meaning of life experiences: the loss of a job is difficult for anyone, but it is engaged with differently by the person who is in her early twenties and negotiating identity within the wider world context, than by the person in his late forties who is struggling with the tension between generativity and stagnation (Erikson). The structural developmentalists provide insight into the way in which the "content" of a given conversation or program is processed and "known" by various people within a particular setting. While it would be a risky and unproductive enterprise to designate the faith stage of any particular person, having insight into the range of stages within a faith community can be enlightening.[69]

It does seem helpful to the religious educator as she or he addresses the range of common themes and questions—Are my children learning the basics? Why has the Church's teaching changed on this? How do we help people feel more connected with the parish?—to be aware of the possible faith stage of the person asking the question. While we might naturally respond from our own faith stance, awareness and sensitivity to the perspective of others facilitates a more effective dialog. The theory of faith development can be seen as providing "scaffoldings of understanding": a helpful framework for recognizing the depth and perspective of the other.[70] There is a way in which these theories of development give us another ear with which to genuinely attend to the other person.

This brings to mind the essential caution that Fowler's stage theory not be used as a means of labeling others. Basically, it is almost impossible to discern the dominant operative stage of another person; outward expression is not helpful in explicating another person's faith stage. Two people may be engaged in similar activities—participating in daily liturgy, contributing time and money in support of issues of justice, or fasting on a regular basis—for very different reasons, and with significantly different understandings of authority and the role of the community. Similar activities can represent different faith stages. So, while labeling a person is unhelpful, having a sense of the faith stages does give us a sense of how the variety of people within a community of faith might respond to a situation or understand a question raised.

In addition to providing potential insights into the perspective of the diverse group of adults within a faith community, these models of development also give an indication of the role of the community itself in the process of growth and development of its members. The role of the faith community in this context can be traced out into three interrelated dimensions.

In the first place is the necessity of the community to be a place of hospitality and welcome to the range of meaning-making stages that are present within the adult community.[71] Essential to this is the recognition of the diversity not only in terms of the "content" supported, but also in terms of the way in which that content is interpreted.

The community also has a role in supporting those who are separating from old meaning systems and embracing new ones. Often this includes an active rejection or a more subtle setting aside of the commitments and relationships that were integral to the old meaning system. The response of the religious educator and the community of faith is crucial at this juncture. Kegan speaks of it in these terms: "The community must be able to serve as a 'holding environment' for *each* developmental meaning-system; if it cannot, the repudiation of an old meaning-system will mean the repudiation of the community as well. For a *religious* community, the challenge is to provide a *religious* holding environment, a support for each meaning-system that resonates to, and makes publicly shareable, its own appropriation of ultimacy."[72]

Third, the community's role is to recognize the continuity of the person in the midst of the change. An analogy: One of the harder transitions for families is not so much when the child leaves for college, but when he or she comes home for summer break. The student sees himself as significantly changed by the experience of the year away; the parents can all too easily remember him as the teenager who broke curfew and needed discipline. In some ways the parents are holders of the memory of the teenager as he passed through prior meaning-making structures. Used to negate the son's nascent system of meaning, those memories are detrimental. But they are put to good use when they help the son to discern the continuity of the new with the old, remembering that he has negotiated change successfully in the past and will again, and to recognize himself within the new meaning system. A successful negotiation of this transition from a family with parents and children to a family with parents and adults can set the framework for the healthful growth of the family into the future. While all analogies have flaws (and I would not want to push the parent-child relationship as an apt analogy for the whole life of a faith community), the faith community can serve as holder of the memory of the members as they have passed through prior meaning-making structures and thus does hold the potential for using the memory of each person to limit development or to enhance it.

FOR YOUR
REFLECTION AND CONVERSATION

1. What ideas caught your attention as you read this chapter? What elements of the chapter elicited strong agreement or disagreement? Explore the reasons for those responses.

2. In what ways is the theory of faith development helpful to your work as a religious educator? How does it inform the work that you do?

3. In what ways is your community of faith a supporting "holding environment" for the complex developing faith of the adults within the community?

4. What implications does this discussion of adult development have for the way in which opportunities for adult formation are organized and facilitated in your setting?

NOTES

1.   Research data from the past decade provide an interesting snapshot of the "average" Catholic and the "average" Catholic parish. But simply in terms of what a Sunday assembly might look like, the statistics reported in *Laity, American and Catholic* give some indication of the population. Among those who are considered "Post-Vatican II" (born after 1960) and identified themselves as Catholic, 24% attend Mass once a week or more, and 36% attend less than once a month. For the "Vatican II Catholics" (born between 1941 and 1960) 45% attend once a week or more, and 21% attend less than once a month. For the "Pre-Vatican II" (born in 1940 or before) 63% attend at least weekly, and 18% attend less than once a month (page 76). Understanding Mass attendance as one of a few significant indicators of a sense of membership and commitment, these numbers give us pause as we think about the demographics of our parishes and the "target" population of present approaches to adult faith formation. William D'Antonio, James Davidson, Dean Hoge and Ruth Wallace, *Laity, American and Catholic: Transforming the Church* (Kansas City: Sheed and Ward, 1996) also James Davidson, et al. *The Search for Common Ground: What Unites and Divides Catholic Americans* (Huntington, IN: Our Sunday Visitor Publishing Division, 1997).

2.   To begin speaking about developmental theorists is to open the conversation to a wide range of resources and perspectives. An important first "sort" of the theories is between those whose foundation traces back to Piaget (structural developmentalists) and those whose work is more reflective of Erik Erikson (psychosocial developmentalists). James Fowler includes a helpful section in his book *Stages of Faith: The Psychology of Human Development and the Quest for Meaning* (San Francisco: Harper and Row, 1981) 37–89. In "Part II: Windows on Human Development: A Fictional Conversation," he brings into dialogue the perspectives of Erikson, Piaget, and Kohlberg. For the sake of the conversation here, which has as its interest the movements of adult faith, these theorists are examined not so much for their entire stage theory but for the contribution that they make to our understanding of faith development theory, and adult faith particularly.

3.   Particularly helpful in understanding the basic concepts of Piaget's schema are two books: Jean Piaget, *Six Psychological Studies* (New York: Random House, 1967), and Jean-Claude Bringuier and Jean Piaget, *Conversations with Jean Piaget* (Chicago: University of Chicago Press, 1980). There is a helpful summary of Piaget's stages in Gabriel Moran, *Religious Education Development: Images for the Future* (Minneapolis: Winston Press, 1983) 58–65.

4.   Kegan presents a convincing argument for the centrality of the process of equilibration to understanding and appreciating Piaget's theory. Kegan argues in *The Evolving Self* that Piaget is significant in his contribution of situating the conversation of development not within the individual alone and not within the press of the environment but in the dynamic of the interaction between the two. "[P]rimary attention [of Piaget's vision], then, is not to shifts and changes in an internal equilibrium, but to an equilibrium in the world, between the progressively individuated self and the bigger life field, an interaction sculpted by both and constitutive of reality itself." (43).

5.   Jean Piaget, *Six Psychological Studies* (New York: Random House, 1967), 7.

6.   Ibid., 8.

7.   In response to a question of why he prefers "equilibration" to "equilibrium," Piaget states: "Because it is a process, not a balance of forces. Equilibrium is a return to the former state. . . . An equilibrated system is a system in which all errors have been corrected, the excesses compensated for. It isn't a static equilibrium like an immobile balance scale; it's the regulating of behavior." Jean-Claude Bringuier, *Conversations with Jean Piaget* (Chicago: University of Chicago Press, 1980), 45.

8.   Lawrence Kohlberg stands as a significant theorist in the discussion of the structural developmental school. He was among the first to move Piaget's schema beyond early adolescents and to examine what it would mean to speak about adult moral development as potentially post-conventional. Although often far too facilely translated into popular form, the philosophical foundation of Kohlberg's theory rewards a careful reading. Some suggestions: *Essays on Moral Development* (San Francisco: Harper & Row, 1981); *The Philosophy of Moral Development: Moral Stages and the Idea of Justice, Essays on Moral Development,* V. 1 (San Francisco: Harper & Row, 1981); *The Psychology of Moral Development: The Nature and Validity of Moral Stages, Essays on Moral Development,* V. 2 (San Francisco: Harper & Row, 1984). A helpful summary of his ideas and critique of his schema is presented in Craig R. Dykstra, *Vision and Character: A Christian Educator's Alternative to Kohlberg* (New York: Paulist Press, 1981).

9.   Carol Gilligan, working within the cognitive constructionist school favored by Piaget and Kohlberg, has raised some serious critiques of Kohlberg's schema from a feminist perspective. Her primary work in this area includes *In a Different Voice: Psychological Theory and Women's Development* (Cambridge, MA: Harvard University Press, 1982) and *Mapping the Moral Domain: A Contribution of Women's Thinking to Psychological Theory and Education*

(Cambridge, MA: Center for the Study of Gender Education and Human Development Harvard University Graduate School of Education: Distributed by Harvard University Press, 1988).

10. Robert Selman examines the social-cognitive process of the developing child. Rooted in a Piagetian framework, he proposes through theoretical and empirical research a four-level schema for examining the evolution of perspective taking. *The Growth of Interpersonal Understanding: Developmental and Clinical Analysis* (New York: Academic Press, 1980).

11. William Perry and his associates examined the way in which college students evolve in their epistemology. They propose a discernible pattern of development for how students "know" or compose truth, a pattern that moves through nine positions within three basic divisions: dualism, relativism, and commitment in relativism. Each stage represents a development in the structures and assumptions about knowledge and how we know. William G. Perry, *Forms of Intellectual and Ethical Development in the College Years: A Scheme* (New York: Holt, Rinehart and Winston, 1968).

12. More attention will be given to Fowler's stages of faith development later in this chapter. Here it is sufficient to say that Fowler's stage theory provides a schema for understanding the way in which the individual's relationships with "centers of supraordinate value" shape the process of meaning making. So when Fowler is speaking of "faith development" he is asking an epistemological question: How does a person's relationship with centers of supraordinate value shape the way in which he or she makes meaning of the world? The primary sources for James Fowler's theory of faith development are James Fowler, Sam Keen, and Jerome Berryman, *Life Maps: Conversations on the Journey of Faith* (Waco: Word Books, 1978), and James Fowler, *Stages of Faith: The Psychology of Human Development and the Quest for Meaning* (San Francisco: Harper & Row, 1971).

13. This acknowledgment that Piaget does not tell the whole story is not a participation in the criticism often leveled at Piaget for presenting a limited and limiting view of human knowing, focusing exclusively on the cognitive dimension. His later writings particularly point to the fundamental connection that he makes between cognitive and affective development. To attempt to apply that critique to those who have followed after Piaget is even more problematic. As we will examine later in the chapter, what is most fundamentally being appropriated by theorists such as Gilligan, Selman, and Fowler is the understanding of the dynamics of development. This is what will be most helpful for our discussion as well.

14. Two primary reference texts from Erikson that are important to understanding his work are his first and his last. *Childhood and Society*, 2d ed. (New York: Norton, 1963) sets out much of the theoretical foundation for his work and presents an examination of the "Eight Ages of Man" in Chapter 7. *The Life Cycle Completed, Extended Version with New Chapters on the Ninth Stage of Development by Joan M. Erikson* (New York: Norton, 1997), serves as a review of

Erikson's thinking on the stages from the perspective of his old age and articulates the place of this theory within psychoanalysis. A helpful though fairly
uncritical secondary source on Erikson that gives focus to the stages but provides access to other elements of Erikson's theory is Francis Gross, *Introducing
Erik Erikson: An Invitation to His Thinking* (Lanham, MD: University Press of
America, 1987).

15. During the 1970s and 80s a good deal was written on adult psychosocial
development; including Daniel Levinson et al., *The Seasons of a Man's Life*
(New York: Knopf, 1978) and, following a similar methodology of in-depth
interviews of a limited number of subjects, the later text *The Season's of a
Woman' Life* (New York: Knopf, 1996). R. Gould, *Transformation: Growth and
Change in Adult Life* (New York: Simon and Schuster, 1978) and Gail Sheehy,
Passages: Predictable Crises of Adult Life (New York: Dutton, 1976). Looking at
the material from a more explicitly education perspective is R. J. Havighurst in
Developmental Tasks and Education, 3d ed. (New York: MacKay, 1972). A helpful article that attempts to trace out the common themes in these theories is
David Wortley and Ellen Amatea, "Mapping Adult Life Changes," *Personnel
and Guidance Journal* (April 1982): 476–82. While each of the approaches to
adult development comes with its own strengths and weaknesses, an overarching and well-acknowledged critique is the almost exclusive focus on the experience of men as normative for adult development. T. Peck proposes an
alternative model for thinking of adult development in women that accounts
for the role of relationship in the process of self-definition among women.
"Women's Self-Definition in Adulthood: From a Different Model?" *Psychology of Women Quarterly,* 10 (1986): 274–84. But even as the scope of theoretical work in adult development broadened to include women, the recognition
of the limited socioeconomic and cultural range of those being interviewed
for the studies was noted. This is particularly true of the research done regarding women's development. See R. S. Caffarella and S. K. Olson "Psychosocial Development of Women: A Critical Review of the Literature," *Adult
Education Quarterly* 43 (1993): 125–51.

16. The central perspective of Gross's reading of Erikson's theory is the way in
which each of the stages either anticipates or recapitulates the forceful dynamics that take place at the adolescent stage. The quest for identity, a key category for Erikson, serves as an essential drive in the activity of human be-ing.
In some ways this is echoed by Kegan in describing one element of the mean-
ing-constructive evolution activity as the need to be recognized.

17. Gross, *Introducing Erik Erikson,* 17.

18. While Erikson's scheme is helpful, too simplistic a universal application
of his theory is problematic. Although argument for its universal application
can be made, there is also the recognition that changes in the sociocultural
context of the individual will have an impact on when each crisis comes to ascendancy. What impact does the extension of school into college and beyond
have on the resolution of one's sense of identity, for example? A more prob-

lematic issue is raised when this model, rooted in research with boys and men, is applied to women. Gilligan, for one, questions the aptness of the separation of intimacy from identity formation, arguing for the essentially relational nature of the process of identity formation among women.

19. Robert G. Kegan, "There the Dance Is: Religious Dimensions of a Developmental Framework," in *Toward Moral and Religious Maturity*, ed. C. Brusselmans (Morristown, NJ: Silver Burdett, 1980), 403–40.

20. His primary reference here is Piaget and those in continuity with his fundamental approach, i.e., Kohlberg, Gilligan, and Fowler. For a clear articulation of Kegan's understanding of the contribution of Piaget see his discussion of the "unrecognized genius" of Piaget in *The Evolving Self: Problem and Process in Human Development* (Cambridge: Harvard University Press, 1982). Central to Kegan's appreciation of Piaget is Kegan's conviction that Piaget's work of defining the cognitive stages has served as a foundation for the recognition of "the process of evolution as a meaning-constitutive activity" (42).

21. "There the Dance Is," 406.

22. Ibid., 407.

23. Ibid.

24. Ibid., 408.

25. Ibid., 411.

26. Ibid., 413.

27. Ibid., 425–26. It is interesting to note that what Kegan speaks about as recognition correlates with the understanding of "identity" that is central to Erikson's theory. Erikson describes identity as "the accrued confidence that one's ability to maintain inner sameness and continuity is matched by the sameness and continuity in one's meaning for others." [Erikson, *Identity and the Life Cycle*, 220] Kegan is pointing to the importance of being recognized as being in continuity across the various developmental eras. He argues for the role of the religious community in serving as a context for that recognition. We will look at that a bit more closely at the conclusion of this chapter.

28. "There the Dance Is," 419.

29. David Tracy, *The Analogical Imagination: Christian Theology and the Culture of Pluralism* (New York: Crossroad, 1981), 160.

30. For Tracy, the limit-to experiences are essential characteristics to the religious dimension of life, and classic religious expressions disclose the limit-of. Tracy writes: "The hypothesis is twofold. First a defining characteristic of the situational 'religious dimension of common experience and language' is the 'limit-to' character of the experience itself, whatever its particular existential focus. Second, a defining characteristic of any explicit religion—more exactly any classic religious expression—is a limit-of character bearing the status of event-gift-manifestation of and from the whole, and experience as giving the respondent wholeness" (165). The implications of this for religious education—particularly the religious education of adults—are significant. At the very least it points to the two-pronged task. On the one hand there is the task

of opening people (including and especially the leaders) to the reality of the "limit-of" character of their experience. This consists primarily of enhancing people's awareness of their experience through opportunities for reflection and conversation. And complementing this is the task of presenting in a disclosive way—through ritual, story, symbol—the potential within the tradition for revealing the limit-of.

31. I question how successful he is in the attempt to bring the two frames of reference together. His early stages (0–3) are essentially linked to the cognitive development set out by Piaget such that movement across these first stages correlates with movement across the stages of Piaget and other Piagetian theorists. See the charting of this in *Stages of Faith*, 52.

32. James W. Fowler, *Stages of Faith: The Psychology of Human Development and the Quest for Meaning* (San Francisco: Harper & Row, 1981), 4.

33. James W. Fowler, "Faith and the Structuring of Meaning," in *Faith Development and Fowler*, ed. Craig Dykstra and Sharon Parks (Birmingham, AL: Religious Education Press, 1986), 15.

34. *Stages of Faith*, 11. Here Fowler is influenced by the thinking of Wilfred Cantwell Smith. In his discussion of the meaning of faith and the distinction between faith and belief (*Stages of Faith*, Chapter 2). Fowler traces the thought of Smith particularly as it is set out in *Faith and Belief* (Princeton: Princeton University Press, 1979).

35. "Faith and the Structuring of Meaning," 25.

36. Ibid., 23.

37. Ibid., 23–24.

38. Fowler develops this in a number of places; here I am following his discussion as set out in "Faith and the Structuring of Meaning," 16–19.

39. Studies in attachment theory in child development give clear indication of the importance of this first set of relationships in establishing the capacity of the child to enter into later relationships. Some of the most significant research can be found in Bowlby, John, *Attachment and Loss*, 2d ed. (New York: Basic Books, 1982).

40. "Faith and the Structuring of Meaning," 17.

41. *Stages of Faith*, 28.

42. Ibid., 18.

43. The clearest and most developed articulations of Fowler's stages of faith are found in *Life Maps and Stages of Faith*, 120–213. The stages are briefly revisited with slight nuance in later works in which he examines the reality of adult faith (see *Becoming Adult, Becoming Christian: Adult Development and Christian Faith* [San Francisco: Harper & Row, 1984] and its implications for a public church and *Weaving the New Creation: Stages of Faith and the Public Church* [San Francisco: Harper, 1991]).

44. *Stages of Faith*, 121.

45. Ibid., 133.

46. Ibid.,137.

47. Ibid., 182.

48. Ibid., 179.

49. Ibid.

50. *Life Maps*, 73.

51. *Stages of Faith*, 183.

52. Helpful in understanding this shift in engagement with the symbolic is the work of Paul Ricoeur. His description of the movement from a "hermeneutic of suspicion" to a "willed naïveté" or "second naïveté" makes clear the critical perspective of Stage 5 interpretation. But for a person interpreting from the position of a second naïveté, there is an embrace of the realization that the critical analysis, which marks a hermeneutic of suspicion, does not disclose all that is present in the symbol. From the perspective of a second naïveté, there is the recognition that the full referent of the symbol can never be revealed; the symbol as symbol must be allowed to speak in its own voice and be embraced on its own terms.

53. *Stages of Faith*, 185.

54. Ibid., 186.

55. Ibid., 198.

56. Ibid., 204.

57. The data from Fowler's research reported in *Stages of Faith* indicates that only one person out of 359 moved beyond Stage 5 to either 5–6 transition or Stage 6 (cf. page 322). Interestingly we hear nothing about this Stage 6 person in Fowler's description of this stage. The rarity of persons embodying a Stage 6 faith in Fowler's study and his tendency to point to very public people whose recognition is as much for their political impact and their rhetoric as their faith perspective raise some serious questions about the validity of this stage and its continuity with the prior stages. The problematic nature of this final stage, described by Fowler as the "normative endpoint, culminating image of mature faith in this theory" (*Stages of Faith*, 199), does raise questions concerning the total enterprise. See John M. Broughton "The Political Psychology of Faith Development Theory" in *Faith Development and Fowler*, particularly 95–97. While I do not think that this critique so weakens the project as to make the theory unusable, there are some issues and critiques, which are discussed later in this chapter.

58. *Stages of Faith*, 201.

59. See "Faith and the Structure of Meaning," 34–35 for such a chart.

60. Fowler argues that he is attempting to bring together the two developmental schools into a more complete understanding of the developing human being vis-à-vis faith knowing. At minimum, Fowler states, he is hoping that his theory effectively highlights the optimal relationship between faith knowing and psychosocial development. (See *Stages of Faith*, 114.) However, while he attempts to draw on the important resources of both schools, he is still vulnerable to the critiques applied to the structural developmental theories.

61. This becomes particularly problematic as Fowler sets out Stage 6 as the

"normative endpoint, the culminating image of mature faith in this theory" (*Stages of Faith*, 199). This is a two-pronged problem: On the one hand it seems untenable to argue that adults who are at Stage 3 or 4 are somehow less people of faith than those at Stage 6. Second, the positing of Stage 6 is problematic—its rare occurrence. Fowler's tendency to draw on historical or well-known personages rather than those whom he has interviewed following the research protocol makes this stage somewhat suspect. This is one of the concerns raised regarding Fowler's Stage 6—the people at the higher stages are often as recognized for their rhetoric as their faith. (See note 58 above.)

62. Fowler writes: "What these stages do offer, however, is this: they provide formally normative criteria for determining how adequate, responsible and free of idolatrous distortions our way of appropriating and living from our particular traditions of faith actually are. The stage theory provides a formally descriptive and normative model in relation to which the adequacy of our particular ways of being in faith can be assessed and faced" (*Stages of Faith*, 293).

63. A similar theme ensues in the discussion of transformational learning in Chapter 3. Do we have a responsibility to challenge a person's meaning perspective?

64. This is discussed in detail in Robert G. Kegan, "There the Dance Is: Religious Dimensions of a Developmental Framework," in *Toward Moral and Religious Maturity*, ed. C. Brusselmans (Morristown, NJ: Silver Burdett, 1980).

65. While his critique of Fowler and other developmentalists appears in several places in his writing, the most coherent and complete articulation of his understanding of this is found in Moran, *Religious Education Development*.

66. See James W. Fowler, *To See the Kingdom: The Theological Vision of H. Richard Niebuhr* (Lanham, MD: University Press of America, 1985), 84.

67. Craig Dykstra, "What Is Faith? An Experiment in the Hypothetical Mode," in *Faith Development and Fowler*, ed. Craig R. Dykstra and Sharon Parks (Birmingham, AL: Religious Education Press, 1986), 55.

68. Maria Harris, "Completion and Faith Development," in *Faith Development and Fowler*, ed. Craig R. Dykstra, and Sharon Parks (Birmingham, AL: Religious Education Press, 1986).

69. An interesting pair of articles appeared in *Adult Education Quarterly* that disagreed about the usefulness of models of adult development for the practice of adult education. Bradley C. Courtenay in his article "Are Psychological Models of Adult Development Still Important for the Practice of Adult Education?" [44 (Spring 1994) 145–53] argues that the lack of clarity of the models, the methodological questions and problems that plague research around developmental theories, the tendency to place value judgments on the attainment of higher stages of development, and the imprecise nature of the implications that one can draw countermand the long-standing position that they are helpful and even essential to adult education practitioners. Responding to the article, Kathleen Taylor in "Why Psychological Models of Adult Development Are Important for the Practice of Adult Education: A Response to

Courtenay" [46 (Fall 1996) 54–62] argues not only for the helpfulness of the theories to the adult educator but the effectiveness of exploring these developmental theories with adult learners.

70. Dwayne Huebner as quoted by Craig Dykstra, "Faith Development and Religious Education" in *Faith Development and Fowler*, 261.

71. The importance of a hospitable and just space to the work of adult faith formation is given further attention in Chapters 4 and 5.

72. "There the Dance Is," 440.

❖ PART TWO ❖

COMMUNITIES OF TRANSFORMATIVE LEARNING

A PARTICULARLY POIGNANT AND PIVOTAL SCENE IN THE MOVIE *Toy Story* has Buzz Lightyear discovering that he is not, after all, a space ranger destined to save the galaxy from the evil empire. He is, in fact, just a toy, a child's plaything. Grappling with this revelation, Buzz searches for alternative ways to make meaning of himself and his place in the world: he attempts to cling to his past vision or to take on the identity that others name for him. Finally, when these fail, he is left with meaninglessness and despair. What saves him in the end, what pulls him from depression to new hope, is the support and challenge of his community. The symbols and values of the community of toys provide the material for constructing a new vision of reality. He embraces for the first time who and whose he is—he is Andy's toy, and that is more than enough.

In many ways the dynamics of *Toy Story* point to core elements that are at the heart of adult meaning making. The characters are called to respond to the vagaries that shape the movement of adulthood—unwanted change, complex relationships, issues of authority, loss of status, disappointment in self and others. Each of the toys deals with all this with various levels of aplomb. In the end, the result is a stronger community, one more accepting, more inclusive, and more able to effectively enter into the opportunities and challenges of life.

Buzz's experience, in particular, points to the fundamental experience that marks the Christian's journey of faith: the invitation to conversion. Like Buzz, all Christians are called to name who and whose we are, and then to align our lives and our energies in response to that identity. And, like Buzz, all Christians are to engage in transformative learning and to do so within the context of a community of faith.

A good deal of research and writing in the area of adult education has focused on the central elements of transformative learning. The writings of Jack Mezirow, Stephen Brookfield, and Patricia Cranton provide rich resources for the process of adult faith formation. While care needs to be taken in bringing categories from other disciplines into the conversation concerning faith formation, there are some rich insights that can be uncovered in that process.

The literature from the business world also has something to offer. The discussion of learning organization that has gained attention over the past decade or more provides a helpful way for us to consider the way in which the community is both resource and location for the ongoing faith formation of its members. The dynamic relationship between the learner and a "learning community" rewards careful attention. These are the themes that are at the heart of Part Two.

3

TRANSFORMATIVE LEARNING: INSIGHTS FROM ADULT EDUCATION

Consider these three stories—anecdotes of people who are entering into a structured process of learning.

Robert has served as a lector in his parish for more years than you can count. And he is a good one: He proclaims the readings clearly and carefully with just enough dramatic flair to gain the focus of the congregation but not so much that he calls attention to himself. He is conscientious about his preparation; he takes time to read the lectionary passages over carefully a day ahead of time. If there is a section that he doesn't understand or finds particularly interesting, he might peruse a couple of commentaries on the lectionary that he has picked up from the local Catholic bookstore over the years. He has actually learned quite a bit about scripture and liturgy in his years of being a lector. He has a

73

sense of the liturgical year and the way in which the readings complement each season's themes. He understands the various genres within the Bible and the importance of applying a historical-critical method to reading the scriptures.

Recently all of the lectors were invited to participate in one of several small groups that will gather to reflect on the Sunday readings. They will meet at various times once a week for an hour; there are a couple that meet at times that are quite convenient for Robert so he agrees to join one for the eight-week commitment. He is looking forward to the discussion, and as he gets ready for the first meeting, he wonders if he should bring one of the commentaries with him.

In the same parish are Jim, Ellen, and their family. While Jim usually goes to Mass with the family on the weekend, he leaves the religious or spiritual formation of their three children to Ellen. So how did he end up having to attend the parent sessions during his oldest son Steven's year of preparation for first Eucharist? He asks that question any number of times as he gets himself and his son ready for the first of a series of monthly Sunday morning meetings. To some extent it is the circumstances of the family—Ellen works as a nurse on weekends and doesn't get home until close to midnight on Saturday nights; their youngest seems to be having colds and earaches with some regularity and Ellen is much better at dealing with that; and their middle son, Ryan . . . Well, Jim doesn't actually know what's going on, but Ryan is having a hard time in school and a hard time getting along with others. It is as though Ryan is

living in his own world. Jim thinks that Ellen
coddles him too much; in fact, Ryan is one of the
major things they argue about these days. So when
Jim and Ellen sat down to figure out how to
accomplish all that needed to be done, Jim
reluctantly took on the task of going to monthly
Sunday morning sessions with his son Steve.

❖

Meanwhile, another parishioner is entering into a
new learning experience as well. Anne teaches
theology to the juniors and seniors in the local
Catholic high school; she is also involved in campus
ministry and serves as the girls' track coach. And
that mix of teaching, ministry, and athletics is a
good blend for Anne. Of all the things Anne does,
she enjoys the senior theology program most.
Designed to help students connect faith with life,
the course brings the Church's social teaching into
dialog with issues of social justice and opportunities for service within the local community and
beyond. Engagement in service projects and
theological reflection on that experience serve as
the heart of the program.

Anne has just found out that she has been selected
to join a group of adults who will be traveling to
Ecuador for two weeks to visit her town's "sister
village." Along with bringing some much needed
medical and educational supplies, she and the others
will be living and working with the people of the
barrio, helping to build a community center that can
serve as school, clinic, and town hall for the people.
Anne is excited about going: she has long taught
liberation theology and topics of social justice. She is
looking forward to seeing these in action!

❖

Each of these people—Robert, Jim, Anne—is setting off on a new learning experience. Each of them brings to this learning past experiences as learner, as adult, and as person of faith. We hope the learning settings they are entering will be ones that are respectful of their past experience and invite them to new learning and transformation. We will return to Robert and Jim and Anne throughout this chapter as we examine ways adult learning takes place and the potential for transformation within the learning process.

A central concept dominating adult education theory over the past ten to fifteen years is that of *transformative learning*. Within adult education writings, this is most commonly traced back to the research of Jack Mezirow. More than twenty years ago, Mezirow examined the experience of women returning to school after a significant hiatus.[1] One of the insights from Mezirow's research was that the ability to engage in critical reflection about the way in which the person viewed the world and her place in it was the most consistent indicator of success in school and after. The women's learning included a "transformation" in their perspective on themselves and others. Interest in the application of transformative learning theory to the general field of adult education developed in the late 1980s and was enhanced by the publication of a number of works on the topic from a variety of perspectives.[2] At the same time that Mezirow's theory was receiving close attention, adult education theorists were also turning to the work of Paulo Freire, an educator from Brazil, for insight into the reality of adult learning. Where Mezirow's work attends primarily to personal transformation, recognizing social change as a possible though not necessary component of transformative learning, the fundamental concern reflected in Freire's work is the process of social transformation founded on the disclosure of systems of power and oppression.[3] These two approaches to transformative learning—Mezirow's and Freire's—and their complementarity serve as central strands to the process of transformative learning that I propose in this text.

The questions we bring to this topic center on the implications of the theory for adult faith formation. Here we focus on an exploration of the fundamental constructs that make up the foundation of transformative learning theory by bringing into dialog the work of Mezirow and Freire. My proposal here is that these theories of transformative learning can serve as helpful resources in constructing an effective approach to adult faith formation and the task of fostering an adult church.

MODES OF LEARNING

All learning is rooted in experience. It is through experience—understood as engagement with one's social and cultural environment—that learning takes place. Experiences that educate provide the person with new insights, understandings, and perspectives.[4] Learning involves "attending to and reflecting on an experience which results in some present or future change in one's behavior, knowledge, attitude, belief or skills."[5]

A child learns to ride a bike through a variety of experiences: her mom explains through words and gestures that the child needs to pedal and balance and keep her head up and steer; the child gets on the bike and takes off with her mom keeping her in balance with a hand on the back of the seat. Eventually, with all those experiences and the multiple experiences of falling over and steering off onto the grass, the child *learns* to ride a bike. This learning is about acquiring *technical knowledge*, knowledge of cause and effect, and of how one relates to and influences the environment.

We gain technical knowledge all the time: how to use a new computer program, how to find the fastest route to work, how to respond sensibly to a child's tantrum, how to run an effective meeting, how to prepare a dynamic class. These are examples of problem-solving learning: we respond to novel experiences by forming a plausible hypothesis for the best course of action and then testing the validity of the hypothesis. The effectiveness of our action serves as the foundational knowledge for the next time we approach the same or similar experience. We have learned through experience.

Our learning through experience, however, goes beyond simply learning how to manipulate and control the world around us. A second form of learning is *practical*, or *communicative, learning*. In this mode the focus is communication: understanding others and having others understand us. Central to this domain of knowledge are social norms and values; interpersonal, political, and philosophical ways of communicating; as well as feelings and reasons. In communicative learning we acquire and convey insights, ideas, and understandings through mutually accepted symbol systems, through language understood in the broad sense to include speech, written word, gestures, images, art, music, and so on. Communicative learning engages us in the meaning-making process of human be-ing, for it is here that we make sense of the world in light of shared world perspectives.

Technical (or instrumental) learning is often inextricably related to communicative (or practical) learning. For example: knowing how to run an effective meeting is connected with instrumental learning, that is, it is concerned with *how* to have an impact on the world. But, knowing *what* makes for an effective meeting is communicative knowledge, that is, it is rooted in the mutually accepted social norms and in the understanding of structures of relationships that are held by the group. Here the subtleties of leadership styles, notions of authority and power, dynamics of group interaction and modes of conversation come into play. It is communicative knowledge that defines what makes for an effective meeting; it is technical knowledge that provides the skills to run one.

These two types of learning—technical and communicative—correspond with the learning we engage in every day. It is through these forms of knowledge that we come to know ourselves, engage in relationships, further our goals, and negotiate and maintain the world as we perceive it.

A third mode, referred to as *emancipatory learning*, is rooted in critical reflection that brings into question the foundations of one's personal and social perspective. In critical reflection people are encouraged to think contextually, that is, to become aware of how their social and cultural environments affect how they think. As children, and even as adults, we appropriate the perspective, or worldview, that encompasses us—from our parents, our peers, and our social structures. We appropriate unquestioningly the presumptions through which our experiences gain meaning and meaningfulness. Emancipatory learning involves an examination of the presumptions that serve to make reasonable the present worldview. Emancipatory learning engages the question *Why?*

To return to the example of effective meetings, emancipatory learning involves moving beyond *how* to run an effective meeting (technical) and *what* makes for an effective meeting (communicative) to ask *why* this type of meeting is considered an effective one in this context and even what we mean by "effective." Emancipatory learning involves a *critical* look at the notions of power and authority and at structures of relationships that define and limit the way in which this particular group meets and comes to decision.

Mezirow describes the process of emancipatory learning in these terms: "The emancipation in emancipatory learning is emancipation from libidinal, linguistic, epistemic, institutional or environmental forces that limit our options and our rational control over our lives but have been taken for granted or seen as beyond human control."[6] Emancipatory learning involves critical reflection through which we are able to recognize inherent distortions, limitations, and narrowness of vision. Emancipatory learning is at the heart of transformative learning and essential to the various expressions of genuinely adult education.

This is not to say that only emancipatory learning is valid or important. There is an essential interconnection among these modes of learning; technical and communicative learning are foundational to emancipatory learning. It is through technical and communicative learning that we gain information, insights, and understanding that serve as the impetus to critically assess the premises and presuppositions on which the meaning of our experiences is based. To some extent, the importance of emancipatory learning in adult education, and specifically in adult religious education or faith formation, is predicated on a presumption about the goal or focus of adult learning. Certainly, acquiring new information and knowledge is often what adults need and what they say that they want. However, as discussed in Chapter 1, the work of adult faith formation is rooted in the church's mission of evangelization. The goal is not simply enhancing membership or helping adults attain more knowledge about the faith; the goal is rooted in adults' membership in an evangelizing community that understands itself to be engaged in the proclamation of the Good News and the transformation of persons and social structures to more clearly reflect God's reign. This vision of adult faith formation necessitates emancipatory learning as a core direction.[7] My contention is that there is a significant intersection where evangelization, transformative learning, and adult faith formation cross paths. And it is at that intersection that the framework for forming an adult church is found.

"HABITS OF EXPECTATION"

To equip ourselves to consider that intersection more carefully, we turn now to the basic structure of transformative learning.[8] Reflecting a constructivist perspective on learning theory,[9] Mezirow understands learning as a meaning-making process that emerges from the way in which experiences are interpreted and reinterpreted.[10] Our interpretation of experience is affected by "habits of expectation" that influence what we perceive, think, and feel, as well as what we *fail* to perceive, think, and feel.[11] These "habits of expectation" serve as sets of assumptions providing a way to make meaning out of an experience but at the same time limiting the interpretation of that experience.

Mezirow examines these "habits of expectation" under two rubrics: meaning perspective and meaning scheme. *Meaning perspective* refers to the broad framework, or worldview, that serves as the lens through which new experiences are perceived and understood. It is "a habitual set of expectations that constitutes an orienting frame of reference that we use in projecting our symbolic models and that serves as a (usually tacit) belief system for interpreting and evaluating the meaning of experience."[12] Our meaning perspectives not only provide a context for perceiving and understanding new experiences, they define and limit what we expect to experience. They serve as filters, allowing us to have easier and more immediate access to those experiences that are consistent with our worldview. They also filter out elements of the experience that are not in keeping with the meaning perspective.

✥

An elderly aunt is buying a birthday present for her five-year-old niece. She loves to shop for her nieces and nephews. Though she does not get a chance to see them often, she tries hard to find gifts that they will like. After wandering the toy store aisles past construction sets and action figures, sports equipment and computer games, she settles on a dainty tea set. If someone were to ask her why she didn't buy her niece the expanded Lego Pirate Ship or a soccer ball, she would say with some surprise, "It didn't cross my mind" or "I didn't even see it."

✥

The aunt's meaning perspective concerning gender roles, shaped by cultural assumptions and past experience, influenced not simply the specific gift that she selected but the total way in which she engaged in the process of shopping for her niece. The aunt's presumption about what it means to be a girl and her tendency to nonreflectively take in culturally defined ideas of the general type of gifts appropriate to a girl are the foundations of the underlying meaning perspective that shapes the way in which she thinks and feels about the task of buying her niece a present. Before she even starts to think about a specific gift, her meaning perspective is already in play, making meaning of the experience and limiting her interpretation of it.

The items she considered to be potential gifts are reflective of the beliefs and attitudes that make up her *meaning scheme.* Meaning schemes, the other meaning structure that Mezirow sets out, are "the specific set of beliefs, knowledge, judgment, attitude, and feeling which shape a particular interpretation. . . . Meaning schemes are specific belief systems."[13] Prior to the shopping trip, the elderly aunt would have been able to tell us that she thinks dolls and games and dress-up clothes are good gifts for her five-year-old niece. She would have been able to state that makeup and nail polish are "too old" for her niece and motorcycle action figures are just inappropriate. These are the components of the aunt's meaning schemes; meaning schemes give particular expression to the generally less-conscious meaning perspective.

Another example:

✥

Susan, a single, childless adult, settles into the pew to read the bulletin before liturgy begins and then tucks the copy in her purse for later reference. Later in the week, a friend who knows of her interest in social justice asks her why she didn't come to the meeting on Tuesday evening. The gathering was the first in a series of evenings designed to explore the core elements of the Church's social teaching and their implications for this parish. Susan looks surprised and says, "I didn't know about it; it wasn't in the bulletin." "Yes it was," her friend responds. "It was listed under 'Opportunities for Faith Formation.'" "Really?" Susan replies. "I must have missed that section."

Susan's expectations are that the faith formation programs are addressed to children and youth, and since she doesn't have children, she seldom even skims that section. Susan brings her set of assumptions—her meaning perspective—concerning parish faith formation into the way she reads and interprets the bulletin. If we were to ask Susan to state her beliefs (i.e., meaning schemes) concerning the goal of faith formation, she could be fairly articulate on what she thinks. Perhaps she would say that it is designed to teach children about the faith; she might be able to name it as part of a larger process of socialization that includes liturgical and communal dimensions of the parish. But her meaning scheme does not include adult faith formation as central to the faith formation process or the notion that all faith formation is to be understood in light of the formation of adults. And if we were to tell her that this was the case, citing appropriate sources and documents, she would perhaps nod and smile and say that it was a wonderful idea. But that alone would not change her meaning scheme, because behind that meaning scheme are powerful meaning perspectives that Susan could less easily articulate. These are meaning perspectives concerning the nature of adulthood, of education. They would touch on her tacitly held understandings of authority and religion and spirituality, understandings that she has garnered from the cultural, linguistic, and personal milieu.

For both the aunt's purchase of her niece's present and Susan's perusal of the bulletin, "habits of expectation" governed what each person saw and thought and felt. And to some extent these expectations or presumptions are helpful. They help us prioritize what we perceive and think about. Without some presumptions about age and gender, the aunt would have no idea what to purchase for her niece: a baby's rattle, a doll, cosmetics, and football equipment would all be equally appealing and perceived as potentially appropriate. Our habits of expectation help us negotiate the world and make decisions effectively and efficiently. But they serve to limit our interpretation of experience as well. And when these presumptions or frames of reference for meaning making are distorted or narrow or inadequate, emancipatory learning is needed to ask why we perceive or think or feel or act the way that we do. This is the essential step in transformative learning, that is, learning in which meaning perspectives are reviewed, challenged, and changed.

In Mezirow's analysis of meaning perspectives, he proposes that there are three different types of meaning perspectives, or complexes of presumptions, that we use to make sense of our experiences.[14] While they are interrelated in practice and in causes of distortion, examining each type can provide a clearer sense of meaning perspectives and the way they are transformed. The first is the *epistemic meaning perspective*, which centers on the way in which we conceive of and use knowledge. Robert, the lector described in the opening story, gains knowledge about the scriptures through careful research and reading good commentaries. He believes that this approach, an expression of a tacitly held epistemic meaning perspective, has served him well in efforts to understand the Sunday readings and proclaim them effectively. Rooted in his past experiences of learning, in his dominant learning styles, and in his scope of awareness, Robert's epistemic meaning perspective relates both to the scope of knowledge and to the way in which knowledge is obtained.

A second type of meaning perspective is related to the social, cultural, and linguistic norms that shape people's understanding of the world. These *sociolinguistic perspectives* reflect the way in which society and language make possible and limit our perceptions and understanding. Rooted in the social milieu, sociolinguistic meaning perspectives consist of those tacitly held ways of making meaning within a particular culture. For example, they shape the experiences Anne and her companions have on their trip to Ecuador. Some in the group see their roles as that of teacher and helper to the people living in their "sister village." With this sociolinguistic meaning perspective, the North Americans understand themselves as bringing the knowledge, skills, and resources to help the people of Ecuador who cannot take care of themselves. Others, hoping to gain much from the trip, are going to be of service and are grateful for the opportunity for exchange and personal interaction. They believe that, in the end, they will learn much more from the people of Ecuador than they can ever teach. Both groups board the plane with their sociolinguistic perspective in tow, and their interpretation of their experiences will be influenced by it.

The final type of meaning perspective is referred to as *psychological meaning perspective*. Forged by the experiences of childhood, these meaning perspectives bear upon the way in which we see ourselves as persons. Self-concept, personality-based preferences, personal strengths, needs, and anxieties: all of these are component elements of our psychological perspective. As Jim gets ready to go to his son's first Eucharist formation program, Jim's understanding of his role in the family, sense of the spiritual dimension of life, and approach to parenting are all reflective of his psychological meaning perspective. His experience of himself is as one who effectively solves the problems that come his way; part of his discomfort and tension around his middle son, Ryan, is that Jim can't solve the problems; he can't make Ryan "better."

One last comment on this discussion of types of meaning perspectives: As is probably clear from the examples, these meaning perspectives are not rigid compartments but interrelated influences of meaning making. The way in which I see myself, while reflective of my psychological meaning perspective, is also shaped by the cultural context within which I live. My being a middle-class, educated, American, Catholic woman are factors that are integral to the meaning perspectives that make possible and limit my perception of knowledge, social order, and concept of self. While naming these three types of meaning perspectives is helpful for analysis, they are not easy to sort out in the case of a particular person engaged in the process of making meaning of her or his experience.[15] I set them out here because I believe that they do point to the complexity of transformative learning and the impact of the multiple meaning perspectives that each person brings to the learning experience.

FOR YOUR
REFLECTION AND CONVERSATION

1. Reflecting on the discussion thus far, name your own insights about the process and place of transformative learning. Do you have anything to add to what has been proposed thus far?

2. Think about a specific experience or decision from the past week: reflect on the "habits of expectation" that shaped your interpretation. This can range from the personal (e.g., what movie you decided to watch over the weekend) to the pastoral/educational (e.g., how you responded to a parent who raised a concern about "covering the basics"). Think about the meaning perspectives and meaning schemes that were in play. How are those categories helpful to you?

3. As you think about the realities and challenges of adult faith formation, consider what meaning perspectives may be operative.

The Process of
Transformative Learning

Essential to transformative learning is the critical examination of the meaning perspectives and meaning schemes upon which the interpretation of experiences is based. Transformative learning involves critically reflecting on these assumptions, recognizing those that are inadequate, and revising them as needed. This is the foundation of transformed meaning perspectives and at the heart of emancipatory learning.[16]

The process of transformative learning is a movement through four moments, each of which is closely related to the others: (1) questioning the present perspective, (2) exploring alternatives, (3) applying the transformed perspective, and (4) reintegrating and grounding of the new perspective.[17]

Questioning the Present Perspective

The process of transformative learning begins with a triggering event or experience that calls into question present meaning perspectives and thus serves as a catalyst for perspective transformation. It is an experience or a series of experiences that expose the present presumptions as not adequate. At times this can be a specific event or experience that does not make sense or that evades easy interpretation; it pushes us to look again at what we know and how we know it. Such an event may take the form of a life crisis: death of a spouse, loss of a job, serious illness, for example. But the challenge to the present perspective can also be more gradual. It can be the impact of a cumulative set of experiences that serve as the impetus to challenge specific assumptions or meaning schemes about self and world. Over time and multiple experiences, there is a challenge of the dominant meaning perspective.

If we look at Robert's experience with the gathering of lectors, we can see the dynamics by which his present meaning perspective is challenged. His approach to scripture reflects an epistemic meaning perspective with an emphasis on the reliability of scholarly research and the role and authority of experts. His premise is that understanding a particular scripture passage is dependent upon understanding its historical and theological significance. The approach of the group he joins reflects a different meaning perspective.

Following a process that allows for a breaking open of the Word in the lives of participants, the questions explored are seldom on the historical or theological significance of the text but rather on its personal and communal significance in the lives of those present and the wider community of faith. The process allows the participants to hear the reading several times and invites them to select phrases or images that seem to draw them into the reading. After a brief introduction to set the Gospel in context, the focus of the time together revolves around discussing these questions: How is this reading Good News for you? In what way does it affirm you and give you renewed hope? How is this story an invitation to you? In what way does it challenge you in how you live and work? How is this Gospel calling you to change and growth?

This approach to considering the Scriptures and preparing to proclaim them at Sunday's liturgy is foreign to Robert and rather uncomfortable. After the second session, he considers dropping out of the group but decides that it is important to follow through on the commitment to eight sessions that he made at the start. And over the following weeks, Robert slowly recognizes the helpfulness of this very different way of engaging with the Sunday readings. If you were to ask Robert to explain the shift or to point to a specific moment when he began to embrace this approach, he would be unable to do so. But by the end of the eight weeks, Robert knew and had experienced that there was more to the Scriptures than a historical and theological significance. His spirituality had been nurtured by the experience, and he willingly signed up for another eight-week commitment.

For Robert the process by which his meaning perspective was challenged was an extended and ongoing one. It was more of an unfolding than a response to a specific event or moment. At some level, the experience of the group put Robert in touch with an unnamed dissatisfaction with his prior way of reading scripture. For Robert, a number of the conditions for transformative learning are present in this experience: he is open to change and new possibilities, the prior way of making meaning in this context has been dissatisfactory, there are others with whom to engage in conversation, and alternative ways of knowing are possible.[18] The potential vitality that this new approach offered served as the impetus for him to explore alternative meaning perspectives.

Exploring Alternatives

At the heart of this second moment in the process of transformative learning is critical reflection on the content, process, and premise of the learning experience.[19] Through this critical reflection we can name the values and assumptions that shaped the prior meaning perspective and begin the process of revising them as needed.[20]

Building on Dewey's notion of reflection,[21] critical reflection involves us in the process of examining the assumptions that have bolstered the way we see and understand ourselves and the world around us. Habermas defines nonreflective learning as what "takes place in action contexts in which implicitly raised theoretical and practical validity claims are naïvely taken for granted and accepted or rejected without discursive consideration."[22] By contrast, critical reflection involves reflection on premises, that is, on the presuppositions that sustain prior learning and interpretation of experience. In ways that echo the writing of Paulo Freire on conscientization, we can say that critical reflection involves questioning the very basis on which the problem or situation is expressed or defined in the first place. Here

I draw on Freire to make more explicit that critical reflection calls in question one's social, historical, and cultural context and the way in which one's context influences perspective. For Freire, critical reflection is in service to changing both one's perspective and the social context that sustains it. I will return to this later in the chapter.

The flow of this second moment of "exploring alternatives" involves us first in critical reflection on our present meaning perspectives; we question their *adequacy* in integrating and framing new experiences and their *authenticity* in respect to our feelings. In light of that critical reflection we engage in exploration of alternative meaning perspectives.

Jim's participation, albeit reluctant, in the first Eucharist formation program with his older son Steve served as an experience of transformative learning. While Jim learned a good deal about the sacramental life of the church and the place of Eucharist in the lives of believers, his most significant learning, while perhaps not intended by the program's planners, focused on his role as parent and as person of faith. In the course of the sessions, Jim began questioning his present perspective (the first moment of transformative learning) as the tension at home with his middle son Ryan intersected with the insights and presumptions of a couple of the people in his small group. Jim was not comfortable with the way he interacted with Ryan. Jim's meaning perspective relating to family roles designated Jim as the one in the family responsible for solving the big problems. Ryan's tendency to be uncommunicative, to withdraw into his own world, has Jim feeling uncomfortable and unsure of himself. He is accustomed to making things "right," and yet nothing he does with Ryan seems to make a difference. So Jim brings into the sessions for Eucharist formation a disquiet with his own parenting and a probably unconscious searching for a way to resolve the situation. Given Jim's present meaning perspective, the resolution is in making Ryan "better"; but the interactions that begin with the Eucharist formation sessions present alternatives.

Three sets of interactions served to invite Jim into a process of critical reflection and then to support him as he examined the values and assumptions that shape his present meaning perspective. The first was the opportunity to talk at some length with parents whose perspectives differ from his. Three or four other men who were regular participants in the sessions gravitated to one another as the sessions began and joined with a couple of others to form an interesting small group for discussion. As the group responded to the assigned questions about children and parenting and faith issues, Jim heard ideas concerning family roles and ways of addressing challenges with children that were significantly different from his. For Jim, a key event was one of the discussion times when a couple spoke freely about the difficulties they were having with their child; Jim was rather surprised by this as he was uncomfortable talking about Ryan to anyone. After some reflection on his reaction, Jim realized that his understanding of himself as the one who solved the problems meant that the continuing challenges with Ryan were a sign of his failure to do his job. This served as an important moment in Jim's exploring alternatives by critically reflecting on his prereflectively held values and assumptions.

The second set of interactions took place in the presentation segment of the Eucharist formation sessions. While it was perhaps most clearly expressed in the session on faith development, the primary themes of all of the sessions focused on the essential connection between faith and life, the importance that adults continue to grow in their faith, and the foundation that parents have already set for their children's faith life long before first Eucharist. While the small group discussion gave Jim the chance to look at his role as parent, the presentation and subsequent reflections provided him the opportunity to examine his role as person of faith.

The final set of interactions took place outside of the Eucharist sessions: they were at home with his spouse, Ellen, in the evening after the kids were in bed. At first these conversations took the form of reports on the Eucharist sessions and passing on any important information. But as the months progressed, Jim began speaking with Ellen more about the insights and ideas and questions that he brought away from the sessions. And over time, when the topic of Ryan came up, Jim didn't immediately begin proposing new solutions but instead spoke about his own reaction to Ryan's behavior and his own fears and concerns. In doing this, Jim was beginning to apply a transformed meaning perspective, one that took him some time to pull together.

Here is one last comment regarding this second moment in the process of transformative learning. It is very difficult, and for many impossible, to engage in the process of reflecting on and critiquing one's present meaning perspective without being in conversation with others. Many people try out new perspectives by talking about them with others or making small steps in hope for affirmation or, at least, acknowledgment. A supportive context in which hospitality and mutual respect are paramount is essential. This is one of several elements that I contend is missing or poorly developed in transformative learning theory as it has evolved in light of Mezirow's schema. While he argues for the place of rational discourse in the process of critical reflection and validating of new meaning perspectives, he gives no attention to the sustaining role of the person's significant relationships, reference groups, and community.[23] We will look at this in more detail in a subsequent chapter as we consider the role of sustained conversation in transformative learning for adult faith formation.

Applying the Transformed Perspective

By the conclusion of the second moment, we have stepped back from our tacitly held meaning perspective, examined the values and assumptions that ground it, and raised questions of the meaning perspective's adequacy and authenticity for us and for our experience. With the next moment we begin to draw and live out implications of the new meaning perspective. And it is just that: a new perspective on our experience, our meaning-making framework. As with any meaning perspective, the new one brings some elements into sharper focus and allows for a clearer view of things that had not been noticed before. For example, in both explicit and subtle ways, the ongoing transformation of Jim's meaning perspective allowed him to see the situation of his son Ryan in a different way and to respond from a different perspective. In addition, seeing himself as a person of faith provided Jim with a new set of lenses with which to view himself and his relationships.

In describing transformed meaning perspectives or meaning perspectives that are more developmentally advanced, Mezirow writes that they are "more inclusive, discriminating, integrative, and permeable (open) than less developed ones."[24] He is pointing to the ability of the more developed meaning perspective to provide for deeper, clearer, and more accurate understanding of experience. It provides a new lens with which to see the world and one's role in it. During this moment, we "try on" the new lenses to see how they fit and how well we can see with them.

Reintegrating and Grounding the New Perspective

This moment can be long and challenging as we begin to integrate the new perspectives into our larger view of the world. There are two elements of that challenge: First, the various types of meaning perspectives, though distinguishable in theory, are interconnected in practice. Robert, the lector participating in a group reflecting on the Sunday scriptures, experienced a transformation in his epistemic meaning perspective. His understanding of the scope of knowledge and the way knowledge is obtained was challenged and changed. But connected to the epistemic meaning perspective are perspectives related to sociolinguistic understandings: Robert's meaning perspectives associated with his view of authority as well as relationship with the Church and its teaching role. As Robert engages with the new meaning perspective played out within the lector group, he glimpses the implications for other aspects of his meaning making.

The second complicating factor is that a significant (or even subtle) shift in one person's meaning perspective has ramifications on the meaning perspectives of others. Coming home from work in the evening, Jim begins to figure out what it means for him to be present and supportive to Ryan by taking time to talk with his son or simply sit with him as he plays with toys or on the computer. While at one level Jim's spouse, Ellen, may appreciate this and even applaud it, on another level this serves as a challenge to the meaning perspective that Ellen has had about her role as mother and advocate for Ryan.

Anne's trip to Ecuador and her return home point to some of the challenges of reintegrating and grounding new perspectives. Anne's fundamental meaning perspectives were challenged in a variety of ways. Because the trip was designed to support the process of questioning present perspectives and examining new ones, plenty of opportunities for personal reflection and group discussion were planned into the schedule. In addition, the rhythm of the days away allowed time for more informal conversation among the participants and between the participants and the people they were working with in Ecuador. Toward the end of the trip, participants were invited to name core convictions and commitments that had taken shape in them over the course of their time away. It was during this process that Anne realized how much she had learned and how much what she had learned challenged a number of ways of doing things that had seemed acceptable before the trip. Her sense of herself and her place within the school where she taught had changed; her sense of her responsibility to do more than expose the seniors to opportunities for service to the community was both exciting and scary. At a fundamental level, she realized that she had been teaching themes of liberation theology in a way that didn't really impinge on her life and decisions. She both hoped and feared that her life would never be the same again!

Anne's return home was disorienting; she found it impossible to just return to things as usual but difficult to convey to others the depth and transformation of the experience. While it was helpful to talk with others who had been on the trip with her, she realized that people she worked and lived with were the ones with whom she would have to express in words and actions her new meaning perspective. From a distance of three or four years after the trip, Anne would be able to recognize the way in which the new meaning perspectives had been integrated into her life and teaching, but the process would not be easy or clear.

Whether fairly smooth and well supported or long and challenging, at the conclusion of this moment within the process of *meaning perspective transformation*, the person has reached an equilibrium in which a new set of meaning perspectives provides a context for interpreting experiences. This equilibrium, or dynamic stability, is maintained until a new trigger event—a new experience or set of experiences that cannot be adequately or authentically interpreted in light of the present meaning perspective—moves the person once again to enter into the process of transformation.

Transformative Learning in Context

This theory of transformative learning provides an important window on understanding adult learning, particularly those experiences of adult learning that open new and renewing visions of ourselves and our place in the world. Those experiences that each of us speaks about as "life changing events" configure in many ways to the movement described above.

As examined thus far, however, our description of transformative learning is not complete; it is, in fact, somewhat one-sided. If one follows the trajectory set by Mezirow, the scope of transformative learning would tend to focus on the rational over the affective and imaginative, the self in autonomy rather than in relationship, and the transformation of the individual over the social. I contend that these three themes constitute core critiques of Mezirow's theory that must be addressed in order to make viable the connection between transformative learning and adult faith formation.

The Rational Versus the Affective and Imaginative

For Mezirow, the process of transformative learning is essentially rooted in the process of critical reflection taking place in the context of rational discourse. Here his overreliance on rationality is evident. Rational discourse serves as the setting for critical reflection, where assumptions and beliefs are questioned, and meaning schemes and meaning perspectives are transformed. Given his description of the optimum conditions of such discourse, Mezirow is referring to a setting in which the participants are independent, rational individuals, unencumbered by external pressure and bound only by the consensus of the group.[25] Without discounting the importance of the rational, it provides only one angle on the process of transformation and transformative learning.[26] There is also an affective, intuitive, creative, and imaginative dimension to transformative learning to be recognized and nurtured in the process of enhancing transformation.[27]

In drawing out the implications of transformative learning for adult faith formation, evoking the role of the affective and imaginative becomes essential. Transformation within the faith context necessitates engaging the imaginative, creative, affective, and nonrational in the process. To illustrate this, I briefly examine three dimensions of adult faith formation that move the discussion of transformative learning beyond the rational.

The first is the place of discernment: while drawing on the rational, there is also an "extrarational" dimension to *discernment* as we look to the myths, images, and symbols of the tradition to find expression of a renewed sense of personal and/or communal vision and direction.[28] In Jim's struggle with a new vision of himself as a person of faith and a new direction for what it means to be parent and father for Ryan and his other sons, the dynamics are not simply rational, though for Jim they do begin there. They are imaginative and creative as he enters into the Christian story and sees Good News there for him and for his family.

A second element of transformation within the faith context is the role of *engagement with the classic texts* of the tradition, particularly but not exclusively the Scriptures, in the process of transformation. We approach these classic texts not for solutions to specific questions or even as sources for propositions on how we are to interact with the world. Rather, it is a case of playing with a text and in the process of interpreting the text, interpreting our lives in a new way.[29] In some ways, Robert has moved from his very rational process of interpreting the text to an imaginative and evocative process of allowing the text to "interpret" him. The transformative learning happens for Robert when he moves from grasping the text to being grasped by it.

Finally, the Christian context brings another significant coloring to the dynamics of transformation: *the experience of conversion.* Whether speaking of a Damascus Road-like encounter with the risen Christ or the ongoing call to conversion that is at the heart of apprenticeship to Christ, most would recognize and even insist that the fabric of conversion, while including a rational dimension, is interwoven with the threads of myths and symbols, of creative connections and, ultimately, of the extrarational "leap of faith." For Anne, the weeks following the trip to Ecuador were difficult not only because she needed to think through a new meaning perspective. They were challenging weeks because, through prayer and reflection, dialog and discernment, she labored to embrace the convictional experience that she had had in Ecuador. [30] In a way that almost defies the rational, Anne knew that her life would never be the same.

These three elements—discernment, engagement with the classic texts, and conversion—are essential to any discussion of transformation within the context of Christian faith and make evident the need to recognize both the rational and extra-rational dimensions.

The Self in Autonomy Versus the Self in Relationship

A significant critique of Mezirow's theory is that it fails to recognize and account for the multiple contexts within which the person makes meaning. "The theory itself, locating perspective transformation within the individual and predicated upon humanistic assumptions of a decisive, unified self, fails to explore the constitutive relationship between individuals and sociocultural, political, and historical contexts in which they are situated."[31] For Mezirow, the participant in rational discourse is the individual who examines evidence and arguments objectively, assesses presuppositions rationally, and stands free from outside coercion or internal self-deception.

As we bring Mezirow into dialog with the Christian perspective seeking insights for adult faith formation, it is clear that there is a conflict in fundamental anthropology. From a Catholic perspective, the "ideal" is not the rational individual in autonomy but the person in relationship. The recognition of the "sin of the world" does not excuse the Christian from seeking to overcome self-deception or social and psychological distortions that prevent us from seeing the world clearly. But it does acknowledge that our vision is always clouded and partial this side of the eschaton and that the ability to see clearly is dependent on *both human effort and God's grace*. The role of the Christian community is twofold: it involves holding the myths, symbols, and stories that serve as resources for meaning making, and it serves as the context for disciplines and practices that make it possible for us to see rightly.[32] All of this needs to be taken into account as we speak about transformative learning within adult faith formation.

The Transformation of the Individual Versus Social Change

One of the most significant and heated controversies related to Mezirow's theory is the relationship between individual transformation and social change. For Mezirow, the role of the educator ends at the point of assisting the individual in the transformation of meaning schemes and meaning perspectives. What the individual does with that transformation, the implications of that transformation for the social and political context, is not the purview of the adult educator in Mezirow's view.[33] Lacking a coherent theory of social change, Mezirow's approach to transformative learning does not engage with the question of political and social action that is part of other theories of emancipatory education.[34] This is a serious lacuna in his work.

Again, the perspective that the Christian tradition brings to this issue insists upon an inherent connection between personal transformation and social change. The way in which we relate and respond to others in charity and justice, and the way in which we establish and support social structures in keeping with Gospel values: these serve as evidence of the authenticity of personal transformation and conversion to Christ. For the educator engaged in adult faith formation, the social and political implications of transformation of meaning perspective in light of the Gospel's call for justice are of central import. Mezirow's limited understanding of the relationship between personal transformation and the reordering of social structures compromises the value of his theory for adult faith formation. As a corrective, I draw upon the insights of Paulo Freire.

Transformative Learning
for Social Change

The writing of Brazilian educator Paulo Freire provides us with a clear point of entrée for the discussion of the inherent connection between transformative learning and the transformation of social structures.[35] In an important way, his writing serves as a central theoretical and methodological foundation for many other adult educators who affirm the essential link between personal transformation and social change.[36]

The conviction that shaped Freire's writing and work in adult education is that education is never neutral. Education can contribute to the maintenance of the present social and political structures by inculcating the dominant group's values so that learners assume that the way things are is the way they are supposed to be. Or it can support the process of liberation by giving the learners the resources to reflect critically on their world and to question the present structure. The latter serves as the grounding for the work of changing society toward a more just and less oppressive vision. For Freire, education must be emancipatory. It must liberate persons and empower them to transform the social structures. The aim of education is to enliven the critical consciousness of the learners so that they are able to recognize the presumptions of the social, political, and economic structures and to take action against the oppressive elements.[37]

Grounding Freire's philosophy of education is his anthropology: Human beings' fundamental vocation is to be subjects engaging their critical capacity and acting on the world to make it a more equitable place. Although dehumanization is always a historical fact, it is not human destiny; the human vocation is a calling toward humanization, and we can be agents in our own humanization. The struggle to overcome alienation and oppression is at the heart of human be-ing. Freire asserts: "To surmount the situation of oppression, people must first critically recognize its cause, so that through transforming action they can create a new situation."[38] The task of education is to support people in that endeavor.

In light of this task of education and the vocation of human beings, Freire articulates his philosophy of education by juxtaposing critique of the dominant model of education—the "banking" concept of education—with emancipatory education. The latter he characterizes as the problem-posing concept of education. A banking approach to education transfers information from the teacher to the learner; the teacher has the information and the student's engagement "extends only as far as receiving, filing and storing the deposits."[39] The teacher is the possessor of knowledge and the student is the recipient; the teacher holds the power in the relationship and the student has none. Given this set of relationships, the banking approach to education—no matter how well intentioned—can only lead to oppression of the students and ultimately of the teacher as well. It may socialize the participants into the existing status quo, but it will not humanize them.

Freire contrasts the banking concept of education with the problem-posing approach that sees knowledge not as a commodity to be handed over but as the dynamic result of human inquiry and conversation. The elements that are at the heart of Freire's model—critical reflection, problem posing, and dialog—are not techniques for the effective communication of knowledge, they are the very way in which emancipatory knowledge emerges.

Given this praxis-based epistemology, the relationship between teacher and student must shift significantly. It is not a relationship of giver and recipient; rather, both are engaged in the process of inquiry that leads to genuine critical knowledge of the world. Freire gives a good deal of attention to the relationship between teacher and student and the necessity of education resolving the "teacher-student contradiction, by reconciling the poles of the contradiction so that both are simultaneously teachers *and* students."[40] Freire's attention to the teacher-student relationship is particularly significant in the face of Mezirow's neglect of this relationship. For Mezirow, the educator is the objective facilitator of the potential transformation of the learner but is in some ways an outsider to the process. That is, Mezirow seems to picture the educator as standing at an objective distance from the dynamics of critical reflection, having the sole task of attending to the optimum conditions for critical discourse. In contrast, the relationship that is at the heart of emancipatory learning—that all are teachers and learners together—must be a foundational commitment of adult faith educators.

A core concept to this problem-posing approach to education is that of praxis epistemology. In its simplest articulation, we can describe praxis as a movement back and forth between reflection and action on the world. A praxis way of knowing involves a series of actions and reflections through which we see the present more clearly and recognize the future that the present is moving toward. It calls us to a critical awareness and analysis of the situation around us, which leads us to evaluate and project the prevailing presumptions into the future for their capacity to humanize the social context. We respond with new action designed to enhance human liberation. In its essence, praxis is not simply a concept related to Freire's approach to education. It is the fundamental way of being human in the world, of shaping the present toward a more just and humanizing historical reality. [41] A praxis epistemology is key to emancipatory education.

Let us now return to the question of transformative learning. As is more than evident from this discussion, the emancipation at the heart of Freire's view of education is from oppressive social, political, and economic structures. While sharing with Mezirow an emphasis on the role of critical reflection for transformation, the purpose of such reflection in dialog with other learners is the recognition of the dynamics of power and the critical awareness of the need for the transformation of society. For Mezirow, the focus is personal transformation that may or may not lead to the individual taking action for social change. For Freire, the focus is social transformation through which the person's reality is transformed and liberated.

In the discussion of transformative learning in adult faith formation, I want to emphasize the importance of both personal and social transformation and the essential connection between them. We need to be careful not to set up a false dichotomy between personal and social transformation. To some extent, the difference is in the dominant lens that the theorist picks up: Freire looks through the lens of critical social theory and sees the need to change social structures that oppress. Mezirow looks through the lens of personal meaning perspectives and sees the necessity to move beyond those that limit our perception of ourselves and our options. Phyllis Cunningham argues clearly for the essential connections between the two:

> To suggest that to educate for personal transformation is somehow not political while social transformation is a political act is to deny the social anchoring of consciousness. To deny personal transformation and to champion social transformation is to deny the unique biography of each person and his or her potential contribution to society and is equally inappropriate. To link personal and social transformation is to construct a polity of democracy.[42]

Bringing these two elements of transformation together is at the heart of adult faith formation and the process of forming an adult church.

FROM ADULT EDUCATION TO ADULT FAITH FORMATION

In this chapter I have attempted to bring into the conversation some of the core concepts of adult education theory, and particularly transformative learning theory, which I believe are helpful for constructing a vision of adult faith formation that enlivens the adult community to deepen their apprenticeship to Christ and to strengthen their commitment to the mission of the Church.

Adult education theory provides categories that can be valuable in our continuing conversation about forming an adult church:

- All learning is rooted in experience—attending to and reflecting on experience mean engaging in technical learning (how to relate to and influence our environment), communicative learning (what the meaning and meaningfulness of the world is and how we convey that to others), and emancipatory learning (what the presumptions are that serve as the foundations of personal and social views of reality and are they adequate).

- Adult education is directed toward all three forms of learning but places particular importance on emancipatory learning. It is through emancipatory learning that personal and social understandings of reality become more inclusive, authentic, and liberating.

- Meaning perspectives—epistemic, sociolinguistic, and psychological—serve as lenses through which we interpret experience. Transformative learning involves examining the sources and premises of these perspectives, evaluating their adequacy and authenticity, and revising as necessary toward more inclusive, authentic, permeable, and liberating ones.

- In general terms we can speak of the process of transformative learning as four moments, each of which is closely related to the others: (1) questioning present perspective, (2) exploring alternatives, (3) applying transformed perspective, and (4) reintegrating and grounding of new perspective.

- At the heart of the process of transformative learning is critical reflection and participative conversation. In stating this, I move beyond Mezirow's model by arguing that to place too much emphasis on rational discourse is to fail to recognize the importance and necessity of extra-rational dimensions to the transformative learning process.

- Transformative learning is shaped by and takes place within a particular historical context. The place of a community as context for sustained conversation and forum for expressing newly articulated meaning perspectives is essential.

- While theories tend to emphasize either personal transformation (e.g., Mezirow) or social transformation (e.g., Freire), my own proposal argues for their intimate and essential connection. To emphasize the personal to the exclusion of the social is to miss the historical context within which we exist and learn; to emphasize the social to the exclusion of the personal is to miss the unique biography that each of us brings to the meaning-making process and the contribution we each make to the transformation of the world.

With these categories in mind, we move to the next chapter that explores the setting and instrument of adult faith formation—the parish as learning community.

FOR YOUR
REFLECTION AND CONVERSATION

1. Reflect on a time in which you experienced meaning perspective transformation. Explore the way in which it transpired; the supports and impediments to the process, both

from within and from others; the long-term effect of the experience; and the insights that reflecting on that experience gives you for approaching transformative learning in the context of adult faith formation.

2. What do you see as conditions within a learning context that are necessary for transformative learning to take place? How are those already present in your teaching setting? How might you enhance or strengthen them?

3. As you reflect on the chapter, what ideas or concepts are particularly important for thinking about transformative learning within the context of adult faith formation?

NOTES

1. Jack Mezirow, *Education for Perspective Transformation: Women's Re-Entry Programs in Community Colleges* (New York: Teacher's College, Columbia University, 1978).

2. Jack Mezirow, *Transformative Dimensions of Adult Learning* (San Francisco: Jossey-Bass, 1991).

3. Of fundamental influence is Freire's work *Pedagogy of the Oppressed,* rev. ed. (New York: Continuum, 1993). For a review of the place of Freire in adult education theory, see Peter Mayo, "Synthesizing Gramsci and Freire: Possibilities for a Theory of Radical Adult Education," *International Journal of Lifelong Education,* 113 (1994).

4. One of the founding voices on this understanding of learning is John Dewey, who wrote during the first half of the twentieth century. In *Experience and Education* (New York: Collier, 1938), Dewey draws out the connection between education and personal experience. While not all experience educates, it is through experience that we learn about the world and the effect of our action in the world. Dewey states that "every experience is a moving force. Its value can be judged only on the ground of what it moves toward and into" (31).

5. Sharan B. Merriam and M. Carolyn Clark, "Learning from Life Experience: What Makes It Significant?" *International Journal of Lifelong Education* 12 (1993), 131.

6. Mezirow, *Transformative Dimensions of Adult Learning,* 87.

7. While I am arguing here that the rearticulation of the mission of evangelization serves as the compelling reason for seeing emancipatory learning as essential to adult faith formation, it is not necessary to have evangelization as the

point of reference to make such a claim for adult education in general or adult religious education in particular. Patricia Cranton, a proponent of transformative learning, states the broader goal clearly: "On the other hand, if we view education as the means by which individuals and societies are shaped and changed, fostering emancipatory learning is the central goal of adult education." Patricia Cranton, *Understanding and Promoting Transformative Learning: A Guide for Educators of Adults* (San Francisco: Jossey-Bass, 1994), 19. Mezirow states it this way: "Not all education involves reflective learning; however, fostering reflective and transformative learning should be the cardinal goal of adult education." Mezirow, *Transformative Dimensions of Adult Learning*, 117.

8.   A helpful review of the literature related to transformative learning can be found in Edward M. Taylor, *The Theory and Practice of Transformative Learning: A Critical Review*, Information Series 374 (Ohio State University: ERIC Clearinghouse on Adult, Career, and Vocational Education, 1998). Reviewing both theoretical and empirical research done in relationship to transformative learning, Taylor discusses many of the unresolved issues related to the topic. He also examines key concerns related to the practice of a transformative pedagogy.

9.   The discussion of Mezirow's constructivist perspective on learning brings us back again to the discussion in chapter 2 of the core human activity of meaning making. From a constructivist perspective, human beings construct the world—that is, they give it meaning. On one hand, this perspective attends to the way in which an individual gains knowledge about the world through the creation of cognitive schemes. (Here, Piaget would be the foundational proponent.) On the other hand, those working from a constructivist framework are also interested in the way in which the person learns through engagement with his or her cultural context. Here, feminist epistemologists serve as a good examples. See Elizabeth Tisdel, "Poststructural Feminist Pedagogies: The Possibilities and Limitations of Feminist Emancipatory Adult Learning Theory and Practice," *Adult Education Quarterly* (1998), 48. For a discussion of central learning theories, see Sharan B. Merriam and Rosemary S. Caffarella "Key Theories of Learning" in *Learning in Adulthood: A Comprehensive Guide*, 2d ed. (San Francisco: Jossey-Bass, 1999). The authors set out five central learning theories, or orientations to how we think about learning: behaviorist, cognitivist, humanist, social learning, and constructivist. Each orientation is founded on a coherent set of assumptions concerning the fundamental purpose of education, the learning process itself, and the respective roles of teacher and learner. Each orientation would also have implications for adult learning.

10.   Mezirow writes: "Learning may be understood as the process of using a prior interpretation to construe a new or revised interpretation of the meaning of one's experience in order to guide future action." Mezirow, *Transformative Dimensions of Adult Learning*, 12. Learning is always given expression in action in the world, understood not as behavior alone but in the larger context of

"praxis." Praxis is construed in terms of the dynamic relationship between reflection and action and "refers to the consciousness and agency that arise from and are expressed in any and every aspect of people's 'being' as agent-subjects-in-relationship, whether realized in actions that are personal, interpersonal, sociopolitical, or cosmic." Thomas H. Groome, *Sharing Faith: A Comprehensive Approach to Religious Education and Pastoral Ministry: The Way of Shared Praxis* (San Francisco: HarperSanFrancisco, 1991), 136.

11. Jack Mezirow, "How Critical Reflection Triggers Transformative Learning," in *Fostering Critical Reflection in Adulthood* (San Francisco: Jossey-Bass, 1990), 1.

12. *Transformative Dimensions*, 42. Mezirow's understanding of "meaning perspective" closely corresponds with the concept of "paradigm." As first described in Thomas S. Kuhn, *The Structure of Scientific Revolutions, International Encyclopedia of Unified Science: Foundations of the Unity of Science*; V. 2, No. 2 (Chicago: University of Chicago Press, 1962), a paradigm serves as a filter through which we interpret and screen sense experiences. Joel Barker has effectively translated the insights from Kuhn and others into an accessible language with application to business. See *Future Edge: Discovering the New Paradigm of Success* (New York: Morrow, 1992).

13. Mezirow, "Transformation Theory of Adult Learning" in *In Defense of the Lifeworld: Critical Perspectives on Adult Learning*, ed. Michael Welton (Albany: State University of New York, 1995), 42.

14. While a discussion of the types of meaning perspectives can be found throughout Mezirow's writing, the most sustained conversation is in Chapter 2, "Meaning Perspectives: How We Understand Experience" in *Transformative Dimensions of Adult Learning*. His discussion of the distortions of these meaning perspectives is found on pages 123–43 of the same book.

15. This is made particularly clear by Cranton in *Understanding and Promoting Transformative Learning*, 40–42.

16. Cranton describes emancipatory learning as "becoming free from forces that limited our options, forces that have been taken for granted or seen as beyond our control." *Professional Development as Transformative Learning: New Perspectives for Teachers of Adults* (San Francisco: Jossey-Bass, 1996), 2.

17. Cranton briefly sets out a number of theoretical frameworks that describe the process of transformative learning. The fourfold movement that we examine here is present in some form in each model. See *Understanding and Promoting Transformative Learning*, 69–76. In light of his early study with women returning to college after an interval away, Mezirow proposed ten steps that he reports have been confirmed by other researchers. See *Transformative Dimensions*, 168–74.

18. Patricia Cranton, *Professional Development as Transformative Learning* (San Francisco: Jossey-Bass, 1996).

19. Mezirow makes a distinction of three types or levels of reflection—content, process, and premise reflection. Content reflection (on what we perceive or think or feel) and process reflection (on *how* we go about perceiving, think-

ing, or feeling) lead to potential changes in meaning schemes. Through premise reflection, the framework—i.e., meaning perspective—that makes our perceiving, thinking, or feeling meaningful is considered. "Premise reflection leads to more fully developed meaning perspectives, that is, meaning perspectives that are more inclusive, discriminating, permeable (open), and integrative of experiences." See *Transformative Dimensions*, 111.

20. Cranton analyzes the differences in the ways in which individuals become aware of values and assumptions and engage with the process of revision. Using Jung's psychological type theory, Cranton explores the strengths and challenges that various configurations of psychological types bring to transformative learning. See Chapter 5, "How Transformative Learning Varies Among Individuals" in *Understanding and Promoting Transformative Learning*, 92–120.

21. For a discussion of Dewey's notion of reflection and the way in which transformation theory builds on and goes beyond this, see *Transformative Dimensions of Adult Learning*, 101–4. As we will see later in the chapter when we look at the contribution of Freire, the notion of reflection and critical reflection derived from Dewey and developed by Mezirow is expanded further by Brookfield to look beyond the personal meaning perspective to examine the social and political structures that support the meaning perspective. Brookfield writes that critical reflection can be seen as being composed of "three interrelated processes: (1) the experience of questioning and then replacing or reframing an assumption, or assumptive cluster which is unquestioningly accepted as representing dominant common sense by a majority; (2) the experience of taking a perspective on social and political structures, or on personal and collective action, which is strongly alternative to that held by the majority; and (3) the experience of studying the way in which ideas, and their representations in actions and structures, are accepted as self-evident renderings of the 'natural' state of affairs." "Tales from the Dark Side: A Phenomenography of Adult Critical Reflection," *International Journal of Lifelong Education* 13 (May-June 1994): 204.

22. Jurgen Habermas, *Legitimization Crisis* (London: Heinemann, 1966), 16; as quoted by Mezirow, "How Critical Reflection Triggers Learning" in *Fostering Critical Reflection in Adulthood*, 10.

23. The category of rational discourse is used in much of Mezirow's writing; see particularly Mezirow's *Transformative Dimensions of Adult Learning* 77–79. Further discussion of the lack of the relational in Mezirow's emphasis on rational discourse is found in Edward W. Taylor, "Analyzing Research on Transformative Learning Theory," in *Learning as Transformation: Critical Perspective on a Theory in Progress*, ed. Jack Mezirow (San Francisco: Jossey-Bass, 2000), 306–9.

24. Mezirow, *Transformative Dimensions of Adult Learning*, 193.

25. Ibid., 77–78.

26. One can argue that given Mezirow's starting point in a Habermasian notion of knowledge, it is inevitable that the role of the rational would have dom-

inance. Beginning with a framework shaped by critical theory, one concludes that the process of transformation involves rejecting inadequate and uncritically accepted frames of reference (meaning perspectives). A different beginning point could make for a process more open to alternative ways of knowing. Scott, for example, argues that, from a beginning point within depth psychology, the process of transformation "focuses on profound emotional experiences that force us to grieve the loss of what used to be a meaningful state of being before we move into another state that is deeper and wiser and more in tune with matter, the body and soul, and the material world." S. M. Scott, "The Grieving Soul in the Transformation Process," in *Transformative Learning in Action: Insights from Practice*, ed. Patricia Cranton, New Directions for Adult and Continuing Education, No. 74 (San Francisco: Jossey-Bass, 1997), 45.

27. A number of theorists and researchers point to this second layer within the process of transformative learning—"the cognitive, rational and objective and the intuitive, imaginative and subjective" (Susan Imel, *Transformative Learning in Adulthood* (ERIC Digest 200, 1998 [cited October 25, 2000]); available from http://www.ericacve.org.docgen.asp?tbl=digests&ID=53. See Taylor, *The Theory and Practice of Transformative Learning: A Critical Review*, 33–35, for a review of the research.

28. See Imel, *Transformative Learning in Adulthood* and Scott, "The Grieving Soul in the Transformation Process," for discussion of the dynamics of discernment outside the specifically religious context.

29. Gadamer uses the image of conversation as a way to speak about the relationship between text and reader, particularly between classic texts and reader. Gadamer's notion of conversation moves beyond the commonplace exchange of information or pleasantries and sees the genuine conversation as a place where the conversation partners are at risk and where the conversation itself takes control. While we may want to say that we conduct a conversation, it is more the case that it "conducts" us. Once establishing the elements of conversation between two people, Gadamer argues that "Everything we have said characterizing the situation of two people coming to an understanding in conversation has a genuine application to hermeneutics, which is concerned with *understanding texts.*" (Hans-Georg Gadamer, *Truth and Method*, 2d rev. ed. [New York: Continuum, 1999], 385.) For Gadamer, and I would argue in the event of transformative learning, understanding comes at the intersection of the world of the text and the world of the reader, a context within which a "fusion of horizons" is possible.

30. A helpful way to speak about this element of conversion is set out in James E. Loder, *The Transforming Moment: Understanding Convictional Experiences* (San Francisco: Harper & Row, 1981). In addition to describing a process of transformation that is similar to the one that I have described here, he expands the notion of transformational experiences by arguing that they are not simply about the person's understanding of the world, but also serve as essential elements of the person's experience of the "Holy" and the "Void." It is interesting

that Mezirow twice makes reference to Loder in his *Transformative Dimensions of Adult Learning*. While tracing out the steps that Loder proposes for "transformational knowing," Mezirow totally misses Loder's anthropology and the dynamic of the relationship between void and Holy which Loder places at the heart of the transformation process.

31. M. Carolyn and A. L. Wilson Clark, "Context and Rationality in Mezirow's Theory of Transformational Learning," *Adult Education Quarterly* 41, no. 2 (1991): 90. In the subsequent issue of the same journal, Mezirow replies to Clark and Wilson by arguing that they misinterpreted his argument for the need for greater self-direction and autonomy of the individual in the process meaning transformation as well as his description of the ideal conditions for discourse. His argument may be valid, and his later work nuances his description of the setting for rational discourse, acknowledging the difficulty in attaining the ideal. See Mezirow, "How Critical Reflection Triggers Transformative Learning," particularly pages 10–12. However, in the final analysis, Mezirow ignores the influence of the social context on the individual's interpretation of experience and reconstruction of meaning perspectives. For him, the ideal remains the rational individual unencumbered by outside influence and able to rationally evaluate, decide, and act. For a review of the literature related to this, see Taylor, *The Theory and Practice of Transformative Learning: A Critical Review*, 25–28.

32. Particularly helpful here is Craig Dykstra's discussion of a Christian anthropology rooted in a recognition of the impact of the sin of the world and the difficulty that human beings have in seeing the world "through God's eyes." Cf. Craig R. Dykstra, *Vision and Character : A Christian Educator's Alternative to Kohlberg* (New York: Paulist Press, 1981) 33–62. While I think that it is important to nuance Dykstra's position from a more explicitly Catholic anthropology, he nonetheless provides an important critique of the generically humanist, rational approach set out by Mezirow. Other resources that can respond to the presumed anthropology of Mezirow include Craig R. Dykstra, *Growing in the Life of Faith: Education and Christian Practices*, 1st ed. (Louisville, KY: Geneva Press, 1999). and Dorothy C. Bass, ed., *Practicing Our Faith: A Way of Life for a Searching People* (San Francisco: Jossey-Bass, 1997).

33. At some level the issue of Mezirow's understanding of the role of the educator also raises the question of his lack of sufficient engagement with the issue of power. His description of critical discourse fails to account for the impact of power within communication. The power of the educator, which is always present in the educator-learner relationship whether desired or recognized by either party, is virtually ignored in Mezirow's work. The question of the role of the educator within adult faith formation is examined in a subsequent chapter.

34. Perhaps one of the most cogent presentations of this critique of Mezirow's theory is presented by Susan and Michael Law Collard, "The Limits of Perspective Transformation: A Critique of Mezirow's Theory," *Adult Education Quarterly* 39, no. 2 (1989). For them this deficit in Mezirow's theory can be traced to his selective use of Habermas.

35. Freire's first book, *Pedagogy of the Oppressed*, originally published in 1970, provided an important critique of the mindset that dominated much of education. His later works expanded the notion of the emancipatory role of education and the place of pedagogy in overcoming oppression. A revised edition of *Pedagogy of the Oppressed* was published in 1993 (New York: Continuum).

36. The appropriation of Freire's constructs and categories by adult education theorists is widespread. At minimum, one can hardly open a book on adult education theory or practice and not find "conscientization" in the index. At a more significant level, a number of theorists have struggled with the foundational contention that Freire has presented: Education is never neutral; it either domesticates or it liberates. (See Sharan B. Merriam and Rosemary S. Caffarella, *Learning in Adulthood*, 2d ed., The Jossey-Bass Higher and Adult Education Series [San Francisco: Jossey-Bass, 1999] 9ff.) However, I maintain that many adult educators appropriate elements of Freire without a thorough understanding of his fundamental frame of reference that personal transformation and transformation of the social structure are essentially connected. The clearest evidence of this is the ease with which some adult education theorists cite Freire and Mezirow in the same context with little indication of the differences between them. (See for example, Cranton, *Understanding and Promoting Transformative Learning: A Guide for Educators of Adults*.) Mezirow's own claim of reliance on Freire is often cited by adult education theorists with little mention of the limits of Mezirow's reading of Freire. In many ways, the differences in anthropological frameworks reflected in these two writers are significant and need to be taken into account. For a discussion of the importance of recognizing the Christian influences in Freire's work see Gillian Cooper, "Freire and Theology," *Studies in the Education of Adults* (April 1995), 27.

37. Freire, *Pedagogy of the Oppressed*,19.

38. Ibid., 29.

39. Ibid., 53.

40. Ibid., 53. Acknowledged but not adequately addressed in Mezirow's work is the question of power within the teacher-learner relationship. This issue will be examined in more detail in the next chapter as it raises significant implications for the relationships of power within adult faith formation.

41. What is probably the most concise and accessible description of the evolution of the concept of praxis can be found in Groome's Chapter 8 "Some Philosophical Roots for a Praxis Way of Knowing" in Thomas H. Groome, *Christian Religious Education: Sharing Our Story and Vision*, 1st Harper & Row paperback ed. (San Francisco: Harper & Row, 1981).

42. John Dirkx, Phyllis Cunningham, Metchild Hart, Jack Mezirow, and Sue Scott, "Conceptions of Transformation in Adult Education: Views of Self, Society and Social Change" (Paper presented at the 34th Annual Adult Education Research Conference, University Park, 1993), 36.

4

FORMING
A LEARNING
COMMUNITY

S everal years ago, the leadership of a parish in mid-Minnesota made the decision to shift the focal point of its faith formation energy from an exclusive attention on children and youth to an inclusive focus on the entire faith community, with particular concentration on adults.[1] Over the next couple of years, a vibrant, creative, and effective process of faith formation evolved that invited all members of the parish community into a shared experience of growing in faith together. As word of it spread to the surrounding parishes, many of us involved in planning and implementing the process were asked to speak about the program and the method by which it was introduced to the parish. My role as theological and catechetical consultant to the process afforded me the opportunity to speak to a variety of people about the presumptions that guided the foundation and development of this adult approach to parish faith formation. While I tended to talk mostly about the vision and rationale, those with whom I was speaking were most interested in the programmatic issues of scheduling, topics, and timing.[2]

One of the most often asked questions was: "How long did it take to put the new program in place?" And my response went something like this: "The short answer is that it took us a just few months. By the middle of January, the parish's religious education coordinator had decided to resign at the end of the year. By the middle of April, after engaging in a national search for a religious educator who could connect with the vision and hope of the parish, it was clear that the best arrangement was to draw on the expertise of people within the parish and design an approach and model that would bring out the strengths of the parish and address its concerns and issues. By the first week in September, we inaugurated our first 'season,' and launched the parish toward a new level of growth in faith and self-understanding that would have an impact far beyond the confines of what we traditionally understood as the religious education program. That is the *short* answer. The *long* answer is that in many different ways, the parish had been preparing for the beginning of the radical shift in its perception of the task of faith formation for quite some time."

In the years preceding the introduction of an adult based model of faith formation, members of the parish had many experiences that influenced their openness to adult learning:

• When the bimonthly lector lists were mailed out, current articles addressing topics related to the lectionary or to contemporary biblical studies were regularly included.

• Each person involved in religious education—the catechists, the assistants, and even the high school "helpers"— received a subscription to a newsletter or magazine that supported them in their own faith journey as well as in their task as religious educators.

• The liturgy committee and other parish committees spent at least half an hour at the beginning of each meeting reading and discussing a recent church document or an article pertinent to their work.

- When waiting to meet with a staff member, parishioners found current copies of *U.S. Catholic, America,* the diocesan newspaper, and other reading material readily at hand.

- The process of building a parish center included regular, meaningful consultation with every level of the parish. People were encouraged to express their opinions and disagreements, arguing forcefully but respectfully for particular points of view. These insights had an impact on the design and use of the center. Several times in the process, binding votes took place at weekend liturgies.

- Finally, in the year or so leading up to the transition, people in informal conversations over coffee, and later in more structured gatherings at the parish, named and acknowledged that the model of religious education in the parish was not adequate for addressing its present and future needs.

All of these experiences, which became part of the fiber of the parish's sense of itself, contributed to its movement toward becoming a "learning community."

While I doubt that anyone (including myself) would have thought to use the term *learning community* in the early 1990s to describe this parish, it was the parish's movement toward incorporating elements of a learning community that made possible the fairly smooth transition from one perspective of parish faith formation to another. And I believe it is by giving form to dimensions of a learning community that parishes and dioceses are most able to give expression to the vision of transformative learning that shapes an adult church into an evangelizing community.

This chapter examines two related themes. The first is the concept of "learning community." Drawing on resources from business and industry that explore the notion of "learning organizations," I make applications to the reality of ministry and parish life and propose characteristics that are at the heart of understanding faith communities as learning communities. The second theme, which closely connects with the first, is the central role of sustained critical conversation in fostering learning communities and in enhancing transformative learning. This theme has been touched on in other chapters; here I present in a more systematic way the elements of conversation and their place in adult faith formation.

LEARNING COMMUNITIES
AS CONTEXT FOR ADULT FAITH

The clear call for adult faith formation and for the creation and strengthening of evangelizing communities is not first and foremost about creating new programs to be added onto existing parish activities.[3] In much the same way that being an evangelizing community is not primarily something a parish does but something a parish *is*, being a community that fosters adult faith is not primarily specific programs that a parish offers but the understanding of lifelong learning that permeates the entire faith community. What needs to be formed is not merely a parish with more programs but a parish that is a learning community.

Insights from Business

Over the past decade the term "learning organization" has worked its way into various aspects of business and industry.[4] Organizations as diverse as automobile manufacturers, healthcare providers, and charitable foundations have found the concept intriguing and challenging as leaders strive to effectively survive and even thrive into the future.[5] While defining *learning organization* is difficult, its fundamental point of reference is the organization as it moves into an ever changing and complex future. According to Senge:

This, then is the basic meaning of a "learning organization"—an organization that is continually expanding its capacity to create its future. For such an organization, it is not enough merely to survive. "Survival learning" or what is most often termed "adaptive learning" is important—indeed it is necessary. But for a learning organization, "adaptive learning" must be joined by "generative learning," learning that enhances our capacity to create.[6]

As Senge indicates, the necessity for all organizations to go beyond adaptive learning to generative learning is rooted in the pace of change in a global economy. Those companies that aim to simply adapt will be left behind; the pace of change requires that organizations creatively imagine themselves into a new future.

Drawing on the work of Margaret Mead, Thomas Hawkins points out the impact of sociocultural change by drawing the distinction between "postfigurative" and "prefigurative" cultures.[7] In a postfigurative culture, the presumption is that the future is in direct continuity with the past, and that the insights and knowledge of the older generation need to be effectively and accurately passed down to subsequent ones. Given the presumed continuity, children learn a limited number of established truths from their elders and that will suffice. In a prefigurative culture, the present is seen as discontinuous with the past; new knowledge is constructed by everyone—young and old—to deal with constant change. Everyone is involved in reconstructing skills, awarenesses, and attitudes in service to enhancing the viability of the society, culture, or organization. In this context, the ongoing learning of all of the members is essential; that is, they need to take on the characteristics of a learning organization.

How does a learning organization come about? What does it look like? At the heart of the learning organization are the five disciplines that Senge argues are the core: personal mastery, mental models, shared vision, team learning, and systems thinking. For Senge, the fifth discipline, systems thinking, is the key and foundation for all the other disciplines.

By discipline, Senge means "a body of theory and technique that must be studied and mastered to be put into practice. A discipline is a developmental path for acquiring certain skills or competencies."[8] Senge makes clear that it is not the case that practicing these five disciplines accomplishes the goal of being a learning organization; a learning organization is not a static reality or an accomplished task.[9] One never "arrives" at being a learning organization, just as one never arrives at being a lifelong learner or an evangelizing community. Practicing the disciplines is not the end point but an opening up to the next step in the process of actively being and becoming a learning organization.

The understanding of learning organizations as set out by Senge, his associates, and others offers the religious educator and pastoral ministers in general some helpful categories for thinking about adult faith formation within the parish and diocesan "organization." At the same time, care needs to be taken whenever we appropriate insights or models from one dimension to another. While some parallels can be drawn across a diversity of organizations, there are, nonetheless, some fundamental differences between a parish and the Ford Motor Company, or Apple Computer, or a major health management organization, for example. Some of these differences have to do with the voluntary nature of one's affiliation to a parish, with the diversity of age and interests, and with multiple ways in which people understand the nature and function of parish. But the core differences have to do with what it means to be a parish and to be a community.

The Parish as Learning "Organization"

The most significant difference between corporate organizations and a parish is grounded in the rationale for striving to become a learning community. Remember that the necessity for becoming a learning organization is rooted in the rapidity of change and the importance of fostering generative learning in order to thrive. Fundamentally, the rationale is pragmatic. But beyond the pragmatic reason for shaping our parishes toward becoming learning communities—i.e., that we can respond effectively to the reality of change—there are core theological foundations for such a move.

By virtue of baptism, all Christians receive the presence of the Holy Spirit and the call to be active participants in building up the Body of Christ and fulfilling the mission of the Church. The conviction is that through initiation, all members receive gifts that are given for the good of the community, and it is incumbent on the leadership and the membership that these gifts be put to good use. Our ecclesiology, which arises from our understanding of the work of the Holy Spirit, affirms that wisdom and insight rest not merely with the designated leaders but within the life of the church as lived by all. So we work to foster genuine Christian learning communities not only as a practical way of effectively addressing rapid change but also because of the defining conviction that the Spirit is alive and active in all members of the community of faith.

From another perspective, it is important to speak about the Christian necessity for ongoing learning. Through initiation, the presence of the Holy Spirit is affirmed; at the same time, the call to discipleship and to apprenticeship to Jesus Christ is proclaimed.[10] In working to be faithful to this call, Christians have the responsibility to continue to grow in their faith and to continue willingly to examine the assumptions about the world that gives substance to their understanding of who they are, who God is, and how God and human beings relate. All of this is part of what it means to be a learning community of faith.

It must be noted that while it appears that we have moved seamlessly from learning *organization* to learning *community*, such a shift is not so simple. Those terms are not synonymous, and the dynamics that shape and inform an organization are not the same for a community. Unfortunately in some of this literature these terms—*organization* and *community*—are used interchangeably and seem to be collapsed. So we can have a comment from Senge: "Once we realize that building organizations is grounded in developing leadership communities, a core question remains: How do such communities form, grow, and become influential?"[11] What is not addressed is the prior question: How are community and leadership community being defined?

Looking at the way in which "community" is described within the Christian context serves as a beginning spot. For Craig Dykstra, for example, the category of "community" serves an important role in the process of faith formation as well as character and moral development. He describes community as having historical, defining dramas, as embodying convictions, and as maintaining a language, symbol system, and forms of common action.[12] While these are central to Dykstra's notion of the role of community, it would not be difficult to find people writing about the nature of organization who would include many of these same characteristics. The question, then, is how do we characterize community?

In the quote from Senge cited above, it seems that either *team* or *group* would suffice for the word "*community.*" There is more to community, however, than simply a group of people working together on a common task; perhaps this description of community is helpful:

> No one can just start a community. Community is analogous to friendship; if you work at it too directly it is not likely to happen, for its nature as gift is not honored. It takes time. A community must have accumulated a pool of significant memories, and it must have forged some compelling shared hopes.[13]

A community has a point of reference outside of itself and beyond the tasks that it intends to accomplish. Like a friendship, it has a shared vision, memories, and hopes that persist beyond a specific task.

In addition, organizations and communities have different perceptions of the role of their members. In an organization the emphasis is on keeping the organization moving smoothly and effectively. The individuals within the organization are fundamentally replaceable. When a sales manager leaves, for example, another one is hired. Although the new employee brings different gifts and may well have a significant impact over time, the learning organization nonetheless continues to exist in its general form through the replacement. The same dynamic is not true of a community, where the fundamental focus is on communication and relationship.

As we speak about the application of learning organization theory to communities of faith, it is important that we be mindful of the distinctive character of community over organization.

The Disciplines: Implications for Parish as Learning Community

Given the centrality of the five disciplines to the expression of a learning organization, it is helpful to examine the way in which they are understood within Senge's frame of reference and then to make applications to the parish setting.

When we speak of the parish as a learning community, we must remember that the referent is the entire parish membership. While the dynamics of a learning community apply particularly to the core staff and the various commissions and committees that serve the parish,[14] a learning community is based on the commitment that all members have to ongoing adult learning.

1. Personal Mastery

Senge describes personal mastery as "the discipline of continually clarifying and deepening our personal vision, of focusing our energies, of developing patience, and of seeing reality objectively."[15] Persons who have developed this discipline well have a clear sense of naming what matters most in their lives and recognizing the core integrity of their lives. They have a sense of what they want to accomplish and are able to attain their goals. To do this, they are committed to being lifelong learners.

Personal mastery is an essential discipline in that an organization's commitment to learning is only as good as the commitment of its members. The person's commitment to lifelong learning in furthering personal goals serves as a foundation to the learning that furthers organizational goals.

As we think of the parish as learning community, the discipline of personal mastery is expressed in the ongoing challenge for all members to examine their lives and goals in terms of a dynamic sense of vocation. Here vocation is not simply about career or lifestyle but is expanded to include all of the ways in which we respond to God's invitation to partnership and faithfulness.[16] Practicing the discipline of personal mastery involves situating the day-to-day decisions a person makes about family, career, finances, and civic roles, within the broader context of the call to discipleship.

For example, the first gathering of those who have indicated an interest in serving as lectors provides the opportunity to invite them to reflect on where this ministry fits into their lives as faithful response to God's invitation. Is this simply another thing to do? Or is there a way in which participating in this ministry is a way of focusing our energies and giving expression to the gifts received in service to the large community? A parish supports the discipline of personal mastery when it provides opportunity for reflection and conversation on the fundamental understanding of the link between faith, life, and personal vision.

2. Mental Models

For Senge, mental models are those often unconsciously held assumptions or images that influence the way we understand the world, make plans, and predict outcomes. As used by Senge, mental models can be understood as synonymous with meaning perspectives and meaning schemes as set out by Jack Mezirow in his discussion of transformative learning.[17] Like Mezirow's meaning perspectives, mental models can be considered inadequate to the degree to which they distort reality, narrow our scope of understanding, or limit our ability to anticipate consequences. The discipline of mental models involves bringing to consciousness the presumptions that we use, articulating their source and implications, and subjecting them to critical examination. We do this through engaging in "'learningful' conversations that balance inquiry and advocacy, where people expose their own thinking effectively and make that thinking open to the influence of others."[18]

In applying this discipline within a learning organization, Senge broadens the lens to include not simply the mental models of the individuals within the organization but the *shared* mental models that define what can and cannot be done in a particular setting, what is and is not the responsibility of a particular group, and so on. It is in articulating and examining these corporately held mental models that the organization can work together to define alternatives.

For the parish as a learning community, this discipline engages not only the specific learner (as transformative learning does)[19] but the entire community of faith. Practicing this discipline involves naming the shared mental models that shape the identity and vision of the parish. Once named, they are examined for their adequacy in supporting the continued growth and vitality of the parish. This seems to be an essential discipline in the growth of parish as learning community. When engaging in this discipline, the often tacit presumptions are brought to light and examined with the goal of defining the nature of the parish—claiming new shared mental models—in a way that is more reflective of the parish.

For example, there are a variety of ways in which the parish serves as a context where cultural, social, and economic diversity meets. The identity of a small town parish, made up primarily of German Catholics whose families have been in the area for generations, is challenged when a sizable tract of very large homes brings in people from the nearby city. In another setting, one of the parishes in an area is closed and its members are assigned to a nearby parish; the differences in priorities and ownership are clear from the start. In a city the regular influx of immigrants finding homes in the low-cost housing district creates a parish where a dozen countries and almost as many languages are represented. In each of these cases, to practice the discipline of mental models, the parish needs to step back and begin to bring to the surface the assumptions that govern its decisions and actions. Engaging in sustained conversation about the sense of parish that people maintain and the implications of that— perhaps in the context of already existing groups such as a liturgy committee or the catechists—is essential for the parish to thrive in this time of change.

3. Shared Vision

Here Senge is not speaking about a vision statement, although those can be important, but rather of a genuine vision that serves to energize and motivate all members and levels of the organization. This vision serves as a point of reference for all the decisions—small or significant—that direct the movement of the organization across time. Building a shared vision is fundamentally about creating shared meaning: "Shared meaning is a collective sense of what is important, and why."[20]

The discipline of building a shared vision involves first encouraging personal vision. Senge writes: "Shared visions emerge from personal visions. This is how they derive their energy and how they foster commitment."[21] While clearly the shared vision is not the sum total of the personal visions, it is incumbent upon the leaders to encourage the members of the organization to both influence and recognize their personal vision within the shared vision.

Conveying the shared vision to the members and teams within the organization is part of this discipline. Senge points out the different attitudes that the people in the organization may have toward a vision—from commitment (sees it not only as the shared vision but as essential to one's personal vision as well) to enrollment (more than willing to sign one's name to it but can imagine the organization without it) to compliance (accepts the vision and sees the advantages, but the vision is outside the scope of one's personal vision).[22] Moving from compliance to enrollment to commitment is at the heart of the discipline of building a shared vision.

For the parish this shared vision is rooted in the Church's fundamental mission to evangelize.[23] While the specific shape and expression of the vision will vary, a clear connection with this core mission is essential. At times the energizing vision may be around a particular element of parish life—enhancing the worship space, addressing specific social concerns, strengthening the mentoring for youth. But in the final analysis, these are always held up to the defining template of evangelization.

Even when the shared vision is clearly articulated, the process of conveying that vision in a way that elicits commitment rather than simply compliance remains the challenge. Key to this, I maintain, is fostering sustained conversation with the goal of engaging as much of the parish as one can in giving shape to the way in which the vision comes to expression. This tends to result in a higher level of commitment and, more important, serves to provide a context for drawing on the wisdom and gifts of the wider parish.

For example: Parish leadership believes that the worship space needs to be renovated. People are invited to town meetings to discuss the options. A large committee is formed to do the necessary planning for the renovation itself, but first they attend to ways to engage the rest of the parish. A process of lectures, small discussion groups, and informal discussions over coffee after liturgies is established. The immediate result is to heighten and bring to the surface some tensions and disagreements over prioritizing the needs of the parish. The long-range effect is to strengthen the sense of parish identity and the conviction that the parishioners have the right and responsibility to engage in the decision-making process. The renovation is put on hold while other issues are examined.

4. Team Learning

As we attempt to name the dynamics of a learning organization, team learning is vital because, as Senge points out, "teams, not individuals, are the fundamental learning unit in modern organizations. This is where 'the rubber meets the road'; unless teams can learn, the organization cannot learn."[24] At the heart of this discipline is mastering the capacity for dialog and discussion and dealing effectively with those forces within the team and outside it that work against productive dialog and discussion.

Dialog, discussion, conversation, debate, discourse: these terms and others point to modes of communication, each having its own focus and goal. While further attention is given to "critical conversation" in the later part of this chapter, it is helpful to draw out the distinction and relationship that Senge and his associates make between productive dialog and learningful discussion.

The purpose of dialog, as Senge understands it, is establishing a context where "collective mindfulness" can be created and maintained.[25] It is the gathering of ideas, insights, and experiences around a particular topic, but not with the goal of coming to a conclusion or solving a problem. The goal of dialog is to enhance the group's way of entering into a topic and to strengthen the members' ability to learn as a team. Productive dialog is dependent on the participants' willingness to engage in attentive listening, to look favorably on the positions or ideas of the other, and to name and examine the presumptions or (mental models) that shape their thinking. Dialog, as understood here, is in service to the pooling of common meaning and collective interpretation.

Discussion is the necessary complement to dialog in the dynamics of team learning. In discussion, positions are set out and defended, alternatives are proposed and examined, and some common agreement on a decision is reached in the end. Effective discussion is characterized by a balance of advocacy and inquiry, that is presenting one's position as well as asking questions of others in order better to grasp their position and bring them to further clarity and cohesiveness.[26]

Recognizing the differences and relationship between dialog and discussion is an essential discipline in team learning. Teams can do this effectively only with extended opportunity for practice.

For the parish there are often few times in which teams—parish council, social justice committee, team of people coordinating some aspect of catechesis—have the opportunity to practice either dialog or learningful discussion. Meetings and gatherings are often highly task-oriented and have agendas that are too long to allow for sustained discussion. One of the consequences of this is that there is no shared vocabulary or meaning, much less common vision and mental models. Establishing a rhythm for all groups that allows for generative dialog and genuine discussions is crucial.

For example, each year the first meeting of the newly constituted parish council is a Sunday afternoon retreat. It begins with the parish liturgy, setting the context of all of the group's meetings within the Eucharist. The agenda for the afternoon is simply to name the positive events that have shaped the parish, the Council, and the members over the past year. In the course of this, participants have the opportunity to engage in dialog with one or two others. Basic characteristics of effective, learningful discussion are reviewed and "practiced" throughout the retreat. The result of this gathering is the foundation of a common set of memories, experiences, and mental models that serves the group well as it moves into the year.

5. Systems Thinking

Designated the "fifth discipline," systems thinking is the essential foundation for all the other disciplines and the conceptual cornerstone of a learning community. Senge describes systems thinking in this way: "Systems thinking is a discipline for seeing wholes. It is a framework for seeing interrelationships rather than things, for seeing patterns of change rather than static 'snapshots.'" He concludes, "And systems thinking is a sensibility—for the subtle interconnectedness that gives living systems their unique character."[27]

A variety of themes coalesce around this discipline of systems thinking; two of them are particularly helpful for our work. The first is the concept of feedback. Given the interrelated nature of any system, actions which we tend to see in a straight line cause-and-effect relationship are in fact part of larger circles in which actions can reinforce or counteract each other; this is the essence of feedback.[28] It is the ever broadening recognition of multiple feedback circles that enable us to see the complexity of the systems within which we function. It also provides a tool for looking beyond the "easy fix" and instead situating the problem within its larger feedback circle.

A second theme that is at the heart of systems thinking is "dynamic complexity." This describes the situations in which the predicted cause-and-effect relationship is subtle and when the long-term outcome of an action is not clear. Senge writes:

> When the same action has dramatically different effects in the short run and the long, there is dynamic complexity. When an action has one set of consequences locally and a very different set of consequences in another part of the system, there is

dynamic complexity. When obvious interventions produce nonobvious consequences, there is dynamic complexity.[29]

For the parish, systems thinking has significant implications. To approach the parish as learning community from the perspective of systems thinking involves moving away from a "silo" approach to parish life. In many contexts the various aspects of the parish—youth ministry, liturgy, school, action for justice, religious education, and so on—are seen as discrete units of the whole that exist side by side but without much interaction. Systems thinking invites and even requires that the interconnection among the various aspects and dimensions of parish life be recognized and that the gifts of all the people be utilized.

For example, the concept of dynamic complexity is helpful when we look at the parish. One of the indicators of dynamic complexity is that there is a difference between the short- and long-term effects of an action. While making sessions for parents in the Eucharist program mandatory may in the short term lead to more adults attending, the long-term effect is to work against the recognition of the role of adult learners in their own learning/formation. While having really engaging speakers who come in with "package presentations" that entertain may in the short run provide for an enjoyable evening, the lack of opportunity for adults to engage with each other around issues of faith leads to a diminishment of the ongoing task of bringing faith into dialog with life. In the short run taking time to study a document in a parish committee means that not as much seems to be getting done. But the long-term impact is to contribute to the creation of a learning community that more effectively incorporates everyone's ideas and insights into the work of the committee. In each of these contexts the dynamic complexity of the learning community requires that we continually rearticulate our vision and respond in a way that furthers it.

While care needs to be taken when applying theoretical frameworks from other contexts to the life and work of the parish, it is clear that there are many elements from learning organizations theory that are helpful and challenging for us. In reviewing the five disciplines and their applicability to the life of the parish, one of the themes that comes to the fore is the centrality of conversation to all effective learning. Senge writes:

> Learning organizations are spaces for generative conversations and concerted action. In them, language functions as a device for connection, invention, and coordination. People can talk from their hearts and connect with one another in the spirit of dialogue. Their dialogue weaves a common fabric and connects them at a deep level of being. When people talk and listen to each other this way, they create a field of alignment that produces tremendous power to invent new realities in conversation, and to bring about these new realities in action.[30]

The nature and dynamics of conversation and its place in the work of adult faith formation is the topic for the next section of this chapter. But first, an invitation to engage in reflection and conversation yourself:

FOR YOUR
REFLECTION AND CONVERSATION

1. What ideas or insights into the nature and functioning of your parish did you glean from this discussion of learning organizations? To what extent do you think the theory of learning organizations is a helpful or applicable one for parish communities?

2. While it is clear that the five disciplines are closely connected, which one seems most important to you as you think about forming a learning community? What elements are present in some form within the parish already?

3. In light of this material, what conviction or commitment about the dynamics of forming an adult church as an evangelizing community have come clear for you?

CONVERSATION AS CENTRAL TO AN ADULT CHURCH

Senge argues clearly that systems thinking is the foundational discipline and the cornerstone of a learning organization; the ability to recognize the feedback circles and the impact of dynamic complexity are crucial for a person, a team, or an organization to learn. While systems thinking is the essential discipline for forming a learning organization, I contend that the essential skill is the ability to engage in sustained critical conversation. It is sustained, critical conversation that makes possible the practice and promotion of the other disciplines. And it is sustained, critical conversation that is constitutive to forming an adult, evangelizing Church.

In this section we look more closely at the nature, dynamics, and role of conversation. Given the central place that conversation holds in my conception of an adult Church, it is evident that the referent for conversation is not the pleasantries we pass with a co-worker while waiting for the coffee to brew, nor the exchange within the family about the events of the day. Conversation as I speak of it here is not even necessarily the late-night interchanges we have with close friends about politics, religion, or the meaning of life. Conversation in this sense takes on specific characteristics. To examine those more closely, we draw on the insights of hermeneutics and particularly the writings of Hans-Georg Gadamer.

Following the explication of the concept of conversation, we can draw out some of the core characteristics of conversation that have particular relevance to the task of catechesis and the work of being and becoming an adult, evangelizing Church. We conclude this chapter by naming some of the significance of this for adult faith formation.

Insights from Hermeneutics

> We say that we "conduct" a conversation, but the more genuine a conversation is, the less its conduct lies within the will of either partner. Thus genuine conversation is never the one that we wanted to conduct. Rather it is generally more correct to say that we fall into conversation, or even that we become involved in it.[31]

With these words, Gadamer opens up a lengthy discussion of the nature and dynamics of conversation that invites us to look more closely at the way in which we come to know and to understand.

What does conversation look like from Gadamer's perspective? In some way we can say that it begins before the conversation itself is under way. In approaching the conversation—whether that is a conversation with another person, with a text, with a piece of art, and so on[32]—we bring with us our prior conceptions, prior knowledge, and prior understanding.[33] These preunderstandings serve to provide the initial meaning to the conversation.

For example, a student comes to me after receiving a fairly poor grade on a mid-term. Since I have met before with students with low grades, I bring my preunderstandings to the encounter. I know what he is going to say—or I think I know, in any case. These become my interpretive frame for beginning the conversation. When he sits down to begin the conversation, I enter into it from the perspective of my interpretive world. Shaped by my past experiences, in this case my past interactions with students, my preunderstandings make it possible to enter into the conversation. I come with preunderstandings that this conversation will be meaningful, that it will focus on a specific topic, and that my role as teacher will be a defining characteristic of the interchange.

While at times those preunderstandings are unhelpful in that they prevent me from understanding the other person, they are, however, essential for the act of interpretation. They serve as the entry point into the "hermeneutical circle." As I begin the conversation, I engage the world of the other person through the lens of my prejudices. The student who initiated the conversation comes with his own preunderstandings and the topic that he is hoping to discuss as well. In genuine conversation, I allow my preunderstandings to be influenced and challenged by the points and insights of the other person. In the conversation with the student, for it to be a genuine conversation, I will need to be open to setting aside my prejudices (preunderstandings) and attend to the world of the student. When that happens, I run the risk of having my preunderstandings challenged; what I thought I knew to be true about the student, about myself, and about the topic we are discussing may turn out to be not true. As this happens, the interpretive circle is completed—my encounter within the conversation has enhanced or challenged or confirmed my interpretive world, adding layers and depth to my next encounter. My preunderstandings both limit and make possible the conversation that I have with another; and that conversation enhances, challenges, colors, or confirms the world of understanding shaped by my experience.

What is the significance of all this? How does it provide insight to how conversation takes place and the role it plays in faith formation? Let me make three points about the nature of conversation from this discussion.

First, in conversation the process of coming to understanding is dependent upon the "back-and-forthness" of the conversation partners.[34] Two parents are talking about the level of education in the children's school. Both use the term *basics*, as in "being sure the children know the basics." At the outset of the conversation, both come in with a preunderstanding of what that term means and what it implies; each simply presumes that the other person understands and interprets the word in the same way. A passing comment to one another and both parents leave content in their conviction that they share a common sense of the basics. It is only in the extended conversation, where one person gives examples of what he means and the other responds with a similar or contrary comment, that the two parents are confirmed in or disavowed of their presumption that the other held a similar position.

Second, while in conversation, my first responsibility is to understand the other and to assist the other in understanding me. Gadamer writes: "Conversation is a process of coming to an understanding. Thus it belongs to every true conversation that each person opens himself to the other, truly accepts his point of view as valid and transposes himself into the other to such an extent that he understands not the particular individual but what he says."[35] There is a listening and a truly speaking that is an essential dynamic of this mode of conversation. I listen with the presumption that the point being made, the position being presented, the insight being articulated make sense and are valid. To the degree to which they do not make sense or do not seem valid, I am caught up short and compelled to look more closely, to name what I am missing in order to gain the understanding that I seek of the other's point of view.

Finally, in light of the first two observations, conversation as it is described here is risky. At one level, self-disclosure in order to assure that the other person comes to understand my point of view is always risky: I may be dismissed or rejected, my ideas may be ridiculed or labeled heretical. But what is at risk in genuine conversation is not merely my pride or standing. The risk of genuine conversation is that I may have to change my thinking. For genuine conversation to take place I need to do more than suspend my presumption that the other thinks the same way I do, or if that proves not to be the case, that the other is probably wrong. I need also to suspend my presumption that I am right!

In a way that brings together many of the elements we have discussed thus far, David Tracy, whose understanding of conversation builds on Gadamer's insights, writes:

> Conversation is a game with some hard rules: say only what you mean; say it as accurately as you can; listen to and respect what the other says, however different or other; be willing to correct or defend your opinion if challenged by the conversation partner; be willing to argue if necessary, to confront if demanded, to endure necessary conflict, to change your mind if the evidence suggests it.[36]

Characteristics of Conversation

Bringing the insights from Gadamer and others concerning conversation into accessible discourse is essential. We have set out what the conversation looks like and named three dynamics that are at its core. We can now bring this one step further by proposing three characteristics that would support this type of conversation particularly in its application to adult faith formation. The conversation needs to be sustained, critical, and marked by mutual respect and trust.[37]

Sustained Conversation

Conversation is "sustained" in two ways: first, in the sense that the amount of time for each conversation is long enough to allow a genuine exploration of ideas; and second, in the sense that the opportunity for conversation is ongoing and an integral part of each gathering of adults. That is, the conversation often continues over a significant period of time and over more than one occasion. This allows for the "back-and-forthness" of a conversation mentioned earlier, which leads to genuine understanding. In addition, it allows the conversation partners to circle back to a topic explored at an earlier time, bringing new insights to bear.

One of the important results of a sustained conversation is that we are able to move beyond the first level of common understanding and polite agreement and truly engage with the differences that are present in any community of faith.[38] In sustained conversation, we have the opportunity to encounter the "otherness" in those with whom we converse. Sustained conversation allows the participants to move through a series of phases that can be described in this way: (1) We use the same words so we must mean the same thing—we have a lot in common; (2) She (or he) uses similar words to mean a very different thing—we have nothing in common; (3) She (or he) uses words to convey the convictions and values that shape his (or her) view of the world—we have much to share and learn from each other.

In addition, sustained conversation gives participants the opportunity to give expression to their convictions, concerns, and questions. I am convinced that one of the reasons that adults are hesitant to talk with others—including their children—about their faith is because they do not have the practice. Understood in this way, conversation helps to clarify our perspective (in being heard, we hear reflected back to us what we said) and provides alternative perspectives against which to examine our own presumptions and convictions. Essential for authentic conversation is allowing our way of seeing and understanding the world to be put at risk by exposure to the difference expressed by others.

Critical Conversation

It is the recognition of difference that serves as a key context for critical conversation. Difference and otherness opens up the possibility of our seeing the world differently. "It is only in allowing our world to be provoked by a questioning that risks the familiar that our world can be enlarged into new possibilities."[39] It is in critical conversation that difference and otherness is disclosed.

Here the focus of conversation is not only the "content," that is, the tradition, the lived experiences of the individuals and the ongoing life of the parish community. In critical conversation, the focus is also on the presumptions or perspectives that make that content meaningful and significant. It is in the critical nature of the conversation that transformative catechesis is possible.

A connection can be made between this discussion of the nature of critical conversation and the work of Jack Mezirow on transformative learning. Mezirow's three levels of reflection—content, process, and premise reflection—can be applied as aspects of the critical conversation. Using Mezirow's categories, critical conversation goes beyond, though it often builds on, questions relating to content, leading to conversation "on what we perceive, think, feel or act upon."[40] It also includes but goes beyond questions related to *process*, which ask about how we came to the particular knowledge, belief, or feeling that we have. Critical conversation moves the focus to the reason, or premise, why the conversation is important. Why is this relevant? In responding to these questions, the conversation enters into the dynamics of transformative learning, in which the meaning perspectives of those involved are named and examined. It is often in conversation with those whose views of the world are different from our own that we can begin to recognize the distortions in our own meaning perspective.[41]

At the heart of transformative learning is the critical examination of the meaning perspectives and meaning schemes upon which our interpretation of experiences are based. Transformative learning involves critically reflecting on these assumptions, recognizing those that are inadequate, and revising them as needed. This is a challenging task because at the heart of meaning perspective distortion is a lack of awareness that we have made an assumption and that that assumption could be questioned. It is primarily in the context of sustained critical conversation that we are able to gain insight into our own meaning perspectives.

A Context of Mutual Respect and Trust

The critical conversation and transformation of meaning perspectives can take place only in a context of mutual respect and trust. This is where the risk of critical conversation comes in— the risk of having your meaning perspectives challenged and thus be required to re-create your meaning-making framework. It is here that the need for attentive listening and careful speaking is required.

In describing the elements of conversation that support mutual respect and trust, Cowan points to the importance of "intentional, disciplined, temporary suspension of concern with one's own position."[42] This does not indicate agreement, but it does set the foundation for a relationship of openness and trust that is essential if the conversation is going to move beyond the initial interchange. And it is this context of trust that makes effective, sustained, critical conversation possible,

Conversation Toward an Evangelizing Church

My contention is that conversation stands as the preferred mode for engaging in the work of catechesis designed to foster an adult community of faith that embraces the call to be an evangelizing Church. The preceding description of conversation sets out for us the direction in which we hope to move when structuring and facilitating conversation with adults. Few of us engage in that level of discourse with much regularity; the challenge of communicating effectively with family and friends around the mundane busyness of life is sufficient. In fact, few adults within the parish communities have the opportunity to engage in sustained critical conversation with other adults about things that matter. Many have seldom, if ever, been invited to talk with other adults about the content of their faith, much less the process by which they came to believe what they believe. In whatever ways we can and every time we can, we have a responsibility to provide opportunity for adults to engage in meaningful conversation.

FOR YOUR
REFLECTION AND CONVERSATION

1. In what way is the image of conversation a helpful one for you? In what ways does it open up your understanding of the work of catechesis?

2. "Adults grow in their faith when they have the opportunity to be in sustained, crucial conversation with other adults about things that matter." Do you agree? Disagree? What question or caution might you want to add to that statement?

3. What conviction or commitment concerning the role of conversation in adult faith formation do you bring from this chapter?

NOTES

1.   The opportunity I had to serve as consultant to the creation and development of an adult-based model that was introduced in the fall of 1990 to the Church of St. Paul in St. Cloud, Minnesota, was one of the most invigorating and vision-transforming experiences of my professional life. GIFT (Growing in Faith Together) played a significant role in enhancing the faith life of the members of the parish and in strengthening the identity and unity of the parish.

2.   See the discussion in Chapter 5 about the relationship among vision, presumptions, structures, and programs in the process of facilitating adult faith formation at the parish level.

3.   See the discussion in Chapter 1 that looks at the call to evangelization as fundamental to the mission of the Church and foundational to understanding the necessity for adult catechesis. Because the Church exists to evangelize, it is of paramount importance that the ongoing formation of the adult community be seen "as the central task in the catechetical enterprise." See Interna-

tional Council for Catechesis, *Adult Catechesis in the Christian Community: Some Principles and Guidelines* (Washington, DC: United States Catholic Conference, 1992).

4. The popularity of the term is generally traced back to the publication of Peter M. Senge, *The Fifth Discipline: The Art and Practice of the Learning Organization* (New York: Doubleday/Currency, 1990).

5. Several of the core resources concerning learning organizations cited in this chapter include many examples of companies and other organizations that have worked to form learning organizations.

6. Senge, *Fifth Discipline*, 14.

7. Thomas R. Hawkins, *The Learning Congregation: A New Vision of Leadership* (Louisville, KY: Westminster/John Knox Press, 1997) 12–13.

8. Senge, *Fifth Discipline*, 10.

9. In an essay reviewing the literature regarding learning organizations, Michael Wonacott points to the debate that exists about the nature of learning organization. For several people writing in the field, learning organization is seen as a concept that is more rhetorical than actual; it serves primarily as an ideal toward which an organization is moving. Wonacott goes on to say, "A common bump in the road to implementation is the idea that the learning organization is a finished product that can be attained, and quickly. This idea is doomed to failure because the learning organization is a developing ability to conduct a continual process—learning, over the long term." Michael E. Wonacott, *The Learning Organization: Theory and Practice* [Internet] (ERIC/ACVE, 2000 [cited 2 Feb. 1, 2001]); available from http://ericacve.org/docgex.asp?tbl=mr&ID=102.

10. The call to apprenticeship that is inherent to initiation is examined briefly in Congregation for the Clergy, *General Directory for Catechesis* (*GDC*) (Washington DC: USCC, 1997). See Chapter 1 for a discussion of this.

11. Peter M. Senge, "Creating Quality Communities," in *Community Building: Renewing Spirit and Learning*, ed. Kazimierz Gozdz (San Francisco: New Leaders Press, 1995), 53.

12. Craig R. Dykstra, *Vision and Character: A Christian Educator's Alternative to Kohlberg* (New York: Paulist Press, 1981), 55–57.

13. Michael Downey, "Community," in *New Dictionary of Catholic Spirituality* (Collegeville, MN: Liturgical Press, 1993).

14. This is examined more specifically in Chapter 7 when those who are engaged in leadership are invited to reflection and conversation about the dynamics of leadership for change.

15. Senge, *Fifth Discipline*, 7.

16. The understanding of vocation that is expressed by James Fowler points to the sense I have here: "Vocation is the response a person makes with his or her total self to the address of God and to the calling to partnership. The shaping of vocation as total response of the self to the address of God involves the orchestration of our leisure, our relationships, our work, our private life, our

public life, and the resources we steward, so as to put it all at the disposal of God's purposes in the service of God and the neighbor." James W. Fowler, *Becoming Adult, Becoming Christian: Adult Development and Christian Faith*, (San Francisco: Harper & Row, 1984), 95.

17. Mezirow describes meaning perspectives as "a habitual set of expectations that constitutes an orienting frame of reference that we use in projecting our symbolic models and that serves as a (usually tacit) belief system for interpreting and evaluating the meaning of experience." Jack Mezirow, *Transformative Dimensions of Adult Learning* (San Francisco: Jossey-Bass, 1991), 42. As an adult educator, Jack Mezirow places at the center of the educational endeavor the work of transformative learning. This learning involves becoming aware of one's meaning perspectives, evaluating them for their adequacy and making changes in them as needed. See Chapter 3 for a discussion of the various forms of meaning perspectives and the process of transforming them.

18. Senge, *Fifth Discipline*, 9.

19. See the discussion of this throughout Chapter 3 where the process of transformative learning involves naming one's meaning perspective and uncovering its influence on how we see and understand the world.

20. Peter M. Senge, *The Fifth Discipline Fieldbook: Strategies and Tools for Building a Learning Organization* (New York: Currency, 1994), 299.

21. Senge, *Fifth Discipline*, 211.

22. Ibid., 219–20.

23. See the discussion of evangelization in Chapter 1.

24. Senge, *Fifth Discipline*, 10.

25. Senge, *The Fifth Discipline Fieldbook*, 359. The concept of dialog appears in many sections of the writings related to learning organizations. Particularly helpful are the fairly sustained theoretical presentation in Senge, *Fifth Discipline*, 238–49; the discussion of the process for setting up dialog sessions in Senge, *The Fifth Discipline Fieldbook*, 374–81. Also Glenna and Linda Teurfs Gerard, "Dialogue and Organizational Learning," in *Community Building: Renewing Spirit and Learning*, ed. Kazimierz Gozdz (San Francisco: New Leaders Press, 1995).

26. For a discussion of the relationship between advocacy and inquiry see Senge, *Fifth Discipline*, 253–59.

27. Ibid., 68–69.

28. Ibid., 73–83.

29. Ibid., 71.

30. Senge, "Creating Quality Communities," 50.

31. Hans-Georg Gadamer, *Truth and Method*, 2d rev. ed. (New York: Continuum, 1999), 381.

32. Much of Gadamer's work deals with interpretation of texts, particularly the classical. Conversation with its common connotation of interchange with another person or persons is used as a metaphor to examine the way in which interpretation takes place. For the sake of our discussion, I am limiting the

focus to interpersonal conversation, as that is the primary (though not exclusive) interest in speaking about conversation in the context of catechesis and adult faith formation.

33. Gadamer uses the word *prejudices* to describe these preunderstandings or fore-conceptions. In doing this he is attempting to reclaim the reality of prejudice in the interpretive process. That is, he is arguing against the Enlightenment position that it is possible to take an objective stance in the task of interpretation and remove one's prejudices from the equation. It is in fact our preunderstandings that make meaning possible in the first place. Gadamer and some of his contemporaries argue that there is no place from which to interpret that does not include our preunderstandings. The best we can do is bring those preunderstandings to the table of conversation and see them as they are. For a discussion of the understanding of fore-structure in light of Heidegger's contribution see *Truth and Method* 265–71. This is developed further in Gadamer's discussion of conversation (383 ff.).

34. David Tracy, *Plurality and Ambiguity: Hermeneutics, Religion, Hope* (San Francisco, Harper & Row, 1987), 11.

35. Gadamer, *Truth and Method*, 385.

36. Tracy, *Plurality and Ambiguity*, 19.

37. Elements of this have been developed in other contexts. See particularly Jane Regan, "When Is Catechesis of Adults Genuinely Adult?" *The Living Light* 37 (2000), 1.

38. Research into the way in which communities grow and evolve gives additional support to the necessity of sustained conversation. Communities begin in a perhaps haphazard way—neighboring homes, children in the same school, members of the same church. Our need to belong, to feel connected, serves to bring this community together. At the next phase, we recognize and celebrate our commonalties. The connections, while growing, are nonetheless at a level where the members are still attempting to define themselves and their place. The final phase is rooted in a mutual sharing of differences. While the phases may be designated with different labels, the researchers agree that the move to the final phase represents the focused, persistent work of sustained conversation. See for example, George Land and Beth Jarman, "Beyond Breakpoint: Possibilities for New Community," in *Community Building: Renewing Spirit and Learning*, ed. Kazimierz Gozdz (San Francisco: New Leaders Press, 1995).

39. Terry Veiling, *Living in the Margins: Intentional Communities and the Art of Interpretation* (New York: Crossroad Herder, 1995) 59.

40. Jack Mezirow. *Transformative Dimensions of Adult Learning* (San Francisco: Jossey-Bass, 1991), 101.

41. See also Patricia Cranton, *Understanding and Promoting Transformative Learning: A Guide for Educators of Adults* (San Francisco: Jossey-Bass, 1994), 168–79.

42. Michael A. Cowan, "The Sacred Game of Conversation," *Furrow* 44 (1993): 30–34.

PART THREE

ADULT FORMATION IN THE FAITH COMMUNITY

THERE ONCE WAS AN OLD MONK, WISE AND HOLY, WHO LIVED IN A monastery set far back in the woods. In addition to being wise and holy, the monk was also considered to be somewhat scattered as he would often go wandering off into the woods and not return when he was expected. His neglect of meals troubled the prior, his neglect of community prayer scandalized some of the brothers, and his neglect of visitors who had come to see him irritated the guest master.

And so it was that one day, after being reminded that he had visitors coming mid-afternoon, the old monk headed off into the woods and did not return in time for his guests' arrival. After waiting for several hours, the visitors decided to walk into the woods themselves in search of the wise and holy monk. They wandered deeper and deeper into the woods. As the light began to fade, they realized that they were lost. In a panic they began to search in earnest, calling the monk's name. Finally, as darkness descended, one of the group stumbled over something and looked down to find the monk curled up under a tree asleep. "We found you!" they exclaimed. "Wonderful! Now you can show us the way out." Getting to his feet the monk replied, "Ah . . . that is a problem. You see, I know many ways into the woods but I am never sure how to get out. If we work together, perhaps together we can find a way out!"

In many ways, Parts One and Two of this book have brought us "deeper into the woods" of what it means to be and to form an adult church. It is with Part Three that I propose a sense of direction for how "perhaps, together we can find our way out."

Gathering the insights from the first parts of this book, Chapter 5 sets out some of the core principles for bringing adult faith formation to life in the parish context. It begins by recognizing the necessity of stepping back from the desire to move too quickly in designing a program or approach. The tendency of many religious education practitioners to look immediately for the program (and often for the textbook or publisher's package) that will address their concerns is problematic, particularly when we are speaking of the paradigmatic shift that is at the heart of the discussion here. Instead it is essential that a parish team or pastoral staff articulate the core vision that guides the faith formation activity of the parish and then name how it will be shaped. From the vision come *presumptions* (principles or guidelines that guide the decision making in planning, implementing, and evaluating the faith formation efforts) and the proposal for *structures* (elements of parish life that contribute to the work of creating a learning community and an evangelizing community). These serve as a firm foundation for creating a program that can respond effectively and integrally to the demands and needs of the adult faith community.

As we think about making the fundamental shift from a children- and youth-based to an adult-based focus, the task can appear, and then become, overwhelming. Where do we begin? How do we get started? These are regular and important questions that arise when parish religious educators gather to speak about giving life to an integrated parish-wide vision of adult faith formation. While the best place to begin flows from the life and issues of the parish, my proposal is that addressing the approach to ministry formation is one fortuitous starting point.

In Chapter 6 I propose a model for catechist formation that is reflective of adult faith theory and is designed to help catechists at all levels—adults, youth and children—to situate their work in the sustaining and life-giving context of the Church's mission. To effectively facilitate a significant shift as is proposed in this book, parish leadership needs to engage in the process with an awareness of the dynamics of institutional change. Resources from business, filtered through the lens of a Christian theological perspective, provide some helpful insights. This is the focus for Chapter 7.

Just as the old monk had discovered that there were many paths that led deeper into the woods, it is clear that there are many paths leading out. These chapters serve to provide some signposts for the hike.

5

ADULT FORMATION: FROM VISION TO PRESUMPTIONS TO STRUCTURES

In an interesting and helpful little book on leadership, Bernie Swain introduces the distinction between "reform" and "renewal."[1] Reform has to do with the structures and external expressions; renewal has to do with conversion. Swain proposes that the work of leadership is to bring reform and renewal together by entering into a three-step process: (1) name the new vision; (2) allow a lengthy period in order to give people the opportunity to explore the rationale for the change, provide opportunity for people to gain the skills and perspective necessary to implement the change, and establish the structures that make the change viable; (3) introduce the reform that gives expression to the renewal. Swain argues convincingly that in the immediate aftermath of Vatican Council II, reform took place without the support of renewal.

Here is an example of reform without renewal. When I was living in Minnesota, the town's commitment to recycling went beyond vague encouragement to the very pragmatic reality that the city required that I buy specially marked bags for my nonrecycled trash. Since recycling entailed no additional cost, I quickly mastered the process because it was financially expedient. Reform had taken place. But, a move to Boston brought a nearby "dumpster," which meant that there was no immediate advantage to recycling. In fact, recycling required that I haul the cans and bottles and papers to a neighborhood center about two blocks away. I returned to a single pail and abandoned the reform.[2] The disadvantage of reform without renewal is clear: The most minor of challenges can derail the best of reforms. Without the conviction and structures that are brought about by renewal, reform has hardly a chance.

I generally concur with the adage that doing something— no matter how small—is better than doing nothing at all. However, when a parish is attempting to give expression to a vision of adult faith formation that genuinely challenges the dominant child-centered view, it is important that a solid foundation be established before programs are initiated. That is, it is essential that reform and renewal go together. Three scenarios highlight some of the issues that arise when we move too quickly to programs.

St. Agnes' Parish: A couple of years ago the director of religious education (DRE) attended a workshop on adult catechesis. Excited and energized by it, she took the opportunity at the next parish staff meeting to speak enthusiastically about the call to adult faith formation. She was ready to put something into place; the rest of the pastoral team, though somewhat less eager, agreed that something should be done. With this encouragement, she set about planning an extensive program including speakers, retreats, and opportunities for Bible study. While advertising was fairly good, few people attended the first two sessions; no one else from the staff participated. Without realizing it, the youth minister planned a meeting of parents and mentors at the same time as the third session. The retreat was canceled for lack of participants; the Bible study never got started. The DRE was really disappointed with the lack of response and put all her energy back into the program for children and youth.

These days, when anyone speaks of adult faith formation or invites her into conversation about *Our Hearts Were Burning Within Us*,[3] the DRE is a reluctant participant. "We tried that," she says. "People here at St. Agnes really don't care about adult programs."

St. Bartholomew's Parish: The DRE and three members of the faith formation committee from St. Bartholomew set about putting into place an opportunity for adult formation. They used as their model a process that had been going well for several years in a neighboring parish, St. Dennis. After attending a couple sessions at St. Dennis, they initiated the program at St. Bartholomew, following the schedule and format just as the other parish had designed it. After the first session, a couple of people voiced dissatisfaction with the schedule, which allowed about twenty minutes for the presentation and an equal amount for small group discussion: they didn't like small group discussion. The folks at St. Bartholomew began to change the schedule without reflecting on the rationale for the original format. By the end of the first year the program consisted of an hour lecture and a brief question-and-answer time where almost no one raised a question. The DRE and committee at St. Bartholomew's were not sure why, but the program didn't seem to have the same energy that it had at St. Dennis.

✤

St. Columba's Parish: The parish staff had been discussing the vision and core presumptions of adult faith formation for a year. Many of the members had gone to a workshop together and came back energized. As they sat down to plan the adult component for the following year, they had before them the structure that had been in place for years—weekly sessions of about an hour with children in groups of about fifteen with one or two adults. They took that structure as given and then began adding elements that they hoped would give life to the vision of adult catechesis. Unfortunately, once the children and youth were assigned space, there really wasn't any good place for adults to meet. And many of the people who would be interested in opportunities for adult faith conversations were already involved in the catechesis of children and youth, and so would not be available for a program built around the present structure. In the end, some new initiatives were put in place, but the sense of an integrated lifelong process that the staff had envisioned didn't come about.

✤

Each of these scenarios points to the difficulties of giving expression to a new vision of faith formation. In each case, some element of the relationship between reform and renewal was in need of further attention. Reform and renewal come together in the movement from articulating vision to naming presumptions to establishing structures and only then initiating programs.

ESTABLISHING A FIRM FOUNDATION

As we move into the discussion of the process for giving expression to a renewed vision of catechesis, two observations serve as helpful prelude. First, catechetical leaders at both the parish and diocesan levels have become accustomed to thinking of changes in catechesis in terms of textbooks and publishers' resources. A group of catechetical leaders exploring together a framework for an alternative way of imagining the catechetical endeavor, almost inevitably have as their first question: "What series do you use?" While the contribution of publishers to the life of the Church and to the work of catechesis is significant, there is a growing recognition that what happens in parishes needs to flow from and respond to the needs of the particular faith community. The role of the publishers is not so much to provide the complete program as it is to set out the best resources and multiple models for adapting the materials to the needs and direction of a specific parish.

The second comment is a corollary of the first: The effective implementation of any catechetical process requires a clear articulation of the strengths and challenges of the parish. An approach that is effective in one setting may not be in another. At the same time, the more that catechetical leaders from various settings gather to discuss models or concepts that have worked for them, the more enriched become everyone's images of what can be done.

With this in mind, we can begin to examine more closely the movement from vision to presumption to structures to program. Like the tip of an iceberg, the program is the element that is visible, that can be appreciated and evaluated by the parish membership; it is within the program that the hard work and careful thought of the parish staff is made evident. However, the viability and effectiveness of planning and implementing a program is dependent upon the often more time-consuming work of articulating a vision, naming the presumptions, and examining the existing structures. Each of the experiences in the parishes described above fell short of the potential because some dimension of establishing the foundation was neglected.

Articulating a Clear Vision

In an article examining the process of change within women's religious communities, Donna Markham writes that leadership begins by tapping into the most deeply held values of the group. Reminding ourselves of the core values—Gospel values—serves to inspire a reimagining of the future and the development of vision. This is the source from which a bold vision can emerge. Markham writes that the role of leaders is this: "Articulate a bold vision and communicate it repeatedly. Such vision must be magnetic and possible. It must inspire and call forth our [faith community's] 'best self.'"[4]

The DRE at St. Agnes entered into the conversation with the rest of the staff with only a sense of the vision that she was following; it was the vision that had been articulated at the workshop, perhaps, but it was not made concrete by the DRE or by anyone else in the parish. Without allowing time for the staff to enter into extended conversation about the place of adult faith formation in the life of the parish and to articulate and "own" a common vision, the DRE is left to "go it alone." This often means that adult faith formation is at the periphery of parish life. In addition, the lack of clear connection between the vision and the program easily led to discouragement when the program didn't go as well as hoped, and to a certain resignation: we tried it and it didn't work.

Naming the Presumptions

While a vision is an essential starting point, it is designed to set out the big picture and the deepest hopes of the participants. Vision statements, when they are reflective of the members' values, are hard to disagree with—they sound and "feel" right. But the vision statement is not designed to serve as an immediate guide for program planning; it is the point of reference, a touchstone of authenticity to which the participants rally. While naming the vision is essential, it is also necessary to draw out the implications of the vision—implications that will serve as the guiding presumptions for establishing the structures and planning the program. It is here that the way in which the vision will come to expression in this particular context is made clear.

What are the presumptions that sit behind the vision for how the future of the catechetical endeavor can unfold? They are the answers we give to these questions in light of the vision: Who is involved? What are we trying to accomplish? How could we or ought we do it? Why should it be done this way? They serve to make clear the implications of the vision statement; until care is taken to set out the core presumptions, the vision's full impact is often unclear. The presumptions for a parish process of faith formation make explicit the guiding principles for the place and shape that it is going to take in the life of the parish. They serve as the basic operating guidelines that play a significant role in determining the way in which time and energy and funds are expended.

All programs are built on certain presumptions; many times these are unnamed and tacitly held. An example clarifies the nature of presumptions and their relationship to the program. Here we can work backward from an existing program and talk about the presumptions that are inherent to it.

Imagine the standard religious education program in a fairly large parish. Besides the pastor and an associate who also works in the chancery, there are a full-time DRE, a part-time youth minister, and a part-part-time person who works with the preschool program. The DRE understands her responsibilities as coordinating the religious education of first graders through adults and working closely with the youth minister on catechesis for high school students. However, if you were to analyze an average week, about 80 percent of her time and creative energy is spent in supporting the programs for children and youth.

It's a good program, well organized and coherent. Children meet in peer groups during the break between liturgies on Sunday as well as on Wednesday and Thursday evenings. They meet in groups of seven or eight children that have been carefully arranged by schools/neighborhoods so that the kids know one another. The series they use is good; one of the reasons it was chosen was the "home activity" sheets that go home with the kids at the beginning of each unit. These sheets give the parents a summary of the unit's lessons and some suggestions about how to work with the central themes at home. The question of whether the sheets are used at home can't be answered. While the DRE had hoped to meet with the parents at the beginning of the year, the meeting didn't work out, so the sheets came home without any preparation of the adults.

The sacrament programs—formation for Penance, Confirmation, and Eucharist—have been given a good deal of attention over the years. They are model programs involving lots of people and with high expectations for the parents. Parents meet monthly for talks on the theme that their children will be studying, and are expected to complete a book at home with them, one chapter a month. There is engagement with the rest of the parish as "prayer partners" for those preparing for sacraments. This is really seen as the core of the program.

Most of the programming for the adults is either periodic in nature or addressed to the formation for ministries. A couple of times a year, a speaker is brought in to address a particularly relevant topic; few people generally attend these sessions. The formation process for ministry attends primarily to the practical elements, with some comments on the place of this work in the life of the Church. As far as adults are concerned, by far the most energy and time goes into the work with parents in sacramental formation.

Even if they did not list their presumptions, we can look at the program and name some of the core ones. These would include:

- The primary focus of religious education is the children and youth, with particular attention given to sacramental formation.

- Children and youth learn best about their faith in peer groups with complementary work done at home with families.

- Families/Parents play a significant role in helping to form children preparing for celebration of first sacraments.

- The primary mode of adult formation is related to adults in their role as parents.

In the process of articulating the presumptions that follow from a newly named vision, it is helpful to begin by considering those that are operative in the present program. Bringing those to light provides clarity to the nature and role of presumptions, and gives a starting point for naming the ones that are more reflective of the vision. In looking at the present ones, we can ask: What presumptions that presently shape the way in which faith formation is done are challenged by the newly articulated vision? Which presumptions are not in keeping with the self-named vision and therefore need to be reconsidered or jettisoned? And which ones are consistent with it and therefore need to be attended to and fostered?

The presumptions, when clearly articulated and carefully modified in the interplay of vision and experience, serve as an important resource in the unfolding of the faith formation process. They act as the criteria for planning, evaluating, and adjusting the parish program.

While change and adjustments in programs are inherent to a living, vibrant process, having a clear sense of the presumptions for the core elements of the program allows the leaders to make changes without losing track of the vision. At St. Bartholomew the lack of clarity and conviction about the core presumptions of the process—in that case that adults learn best in sustained conversation with other adults—led to changes that actually worked against the articulated vision.

Examining Structures

Once the presumptions are named and affirmed by those involved, particularly the wider parish leadership, the next move is to look at the structures within the parish that would support giving expression to the vision and presumptions. By structure, I am referring to two different though related dynamics in the life of the parish.

The first set of issues relates to how the life of the parish is structured. Here we ask about the way in which various elements of parish life are or could be in relationship with one another: What is the web of communication and interaction in the parish community? How does the pastoral team or staff support each other in the various parish activities? What is the relationship between those involved in liturgy and those involved in catechesis? How do the social committee and the social justice committee engage in conversation with one another? Where and how do adults already gather for conversation within the dynamics of parish life? In essence, all of these questions are asking about the structure and dynamics of relationships within the parish that contribute to the vision and reflect the presumptions set out.

A second set of issues involves looking more specifically at the parish's catechetical program and asking questions about what structures control the direction in which the parish moves in giving life to the vision. Here I am thinking of structure in terms of time and place. Does the scheduling of meetings and children's classes afford the optimum opportunity for adults to gather? Does it make clear the fundamental connection of faith formation to the life and vitality of the parish? Does it give enough time for genuine conversation? How do the facilities affect the way in which the presumptions will be given expression?

St. Columba's had started off well by investing time and energy in talking about the vision and naming some of the presumptions that flowed from the vision. But they didn't step back to look at the structures that were already present in the parish and to evaluate them against the vision and presumptions. The structures in place for children simply could not support the work with adults. The result was a solid vision but no structures to support the program.

Before looking briefly at program, it is important to note that when we examine structures and programs we need to do so with an eye toward "holding on and letting go." That is, we must hold on to those elements that are in keeping with the vision statement and support the presumptions that have been articulated while letting go of those that are not.[5] Without "letting go" of elements that are not in support of the vision and presumptions, mind-sets and approaches that are contrary to the hoped for movement of the parish are not challenged. In addition, by not attending to the movement of holding on and letting go, there is a tendency to simply add more things: Bible study and couples' groups and periodic lecture series. Adding these without examining the structure and presumptions behind them leads to an accumulation of disparate activities and the dissipation of the energy of the leadership. And finally, without "holding on" it is possible to miss some of the ways in which the parish is already working toward this vision. Holding on and enhancing the appropriate elements of the catechetical work of the church gives the opportunity to establish additional and potentially more effective structures of relationship within the parish: How does the process of Christian initiation of adults fit in with the ongoing program of adult formation? How can the post-Confirmation youth support the faith growth of the junior high group? How are the sacramental formation programs for parents genuinely experiences of adult faith formation? A careful consideration of these kinds of questions serves as a solid foundation for establishing an integrated, coherent, and unified experience of faith formation for all members of the parish community.

Initiating the Program

As was discussed in Chapter 4, the call for adult faith formation that we find in Church documents is not simply a call for more individual programs for adults, but an affirmation of the creation of learning communities. So even as we speak about initiating programs, it is essential that the wider view of forming an evangelizing community be maintained.

We can think of the planning process as having two core elements: remote and immediate. The remote planning consists of naming or establishing the needed structures, determining the specific format of the sessions, and defining their focus and direction. It is in the process of remote planning that the people who are working with the program—catechists, facilitators, and so on—are gathered and formed into a sense of their identity and place in the life of the community.[6] It is also often in this context that more communication with the wider parish community takes place. While invited into the process at every level, it is as the program takes shape that people are given further information and called to active participation.

Immediate planning centers on attending to the details that are in service to the smooth and hospitable experience of a particular session. We can think of this part of the planning process as similar to the role that a host plays in giving a dinner party.[7] The host plans the menu in light of the needs and preferences of those invited; she prepares the food and the environment in a way that is aesthetically pleasing; and she plans the evening with the understanding that the conversations that ensue must be allowed to unfold on their own without undue direction from her. In a similar way, the person directing a program plans the evening so that the issues and experiences of the participants are brought into dialog with the sessions topic and direction; she arranges the environment to enhance the dynamics of the evening; and she recognizes that the multilayered conversation that defines the movement of the evening will unfold in ways she can't even imagine.

A PROPOSAL: VISION AND PRESUMPTIONS

In many ways the strengths and resources of the particular parish fundamentally determine the structure and program. The availability of a parish center where people can gather in small groups; a close sense of neighborhood with small communities naturally gathering around shared interests; a nearby Catholic college or university from which to draw speakers and teachers; the financial ability to purchase published resources: the presence (or absence) of these structural realities influence the direction a parish takes as it moves from structures to program.

When we look at the process for determining vision and presumptions, however, it becomes clear that these are not simply determined by a parish in relative isolation. They emerge from the dynamic interaction of many perspectives including the overall vision of the parish, the goal of catechesis as understood both locally and in the wider context of ecclesial documents, the understanding of faith development, adult education theory, and, most centrally, the mission of the Church. So while program and structure are appropriately determined at a parish level, the defining of presumptions and vision, while taking place within the parish, must reflect an awareness of the broader context.

In many ways the first four chapters of this book are about defining the broader context within which a parish's catechetical

vision and presumptions are defined. With those as the back-
drop, let me here propose elements of a vision as well as a series
of presumptions that can serve as a starting point for the further conversation and refinement that need to take place at the
parish level.

Elements of a Vision

At its most integral, adult catechesis provides participants with
the means and perspectives that allow them to give expression to
their baptism through engagement with the mission of evangelization. While we want and encourage an active sense of membership expressed in service to the community of faith,
ultimately, the Church is gathered to be sent, and the most important expression of the reality of the Church is its commitment to transform the world in light of the reign of God. So, a
vision statement for catechesis has as its central point of depar-
ture the mission of the Church that is to proclaim the reign of
God: the reality of God's action in human history. This is at the
heart of the common call to be an evangelizing community.[8]

Rooted in baptism, the work of evangelization is grounded
in the person's relationship to Jesus Christ. "The definitive aim
of catechesis is to put people not only in touch, but also in communion and intimacy, with Jesus Christ" (*GDC* 80).[9] While personal in nature, the relationship with Jesus is not individual: We
are called into communion with Jesus Christ in the context of
the community of faith. It is within the faith community that
each person's relationship with Jesus is defined and strengthened. So a vision statement also includes this fundamental al-
liance between personal faith and the faith of the community.
It is within the context of the community of faith that each of us
receives and gives expression to the call to be evangelizers.

In light of this, a proposed vision statement might begin:
"Catechesis challenges, prepares, and motivates the full commu-

nity of faith to give expression to the relationship to Jesus Christ in active engagement with the Church's mission of evangelization." This is a formidable vision, no doubt, but one worthy of our best efforts and our best resources, for nothing less than the fulfillment of the Church's identity and the effective proclamation of the liberating work of God in Jesus Christ is in play.

Proposed Presumptions

The fundamental elements of the vision provide a starting point. A series of five presumptions serves to draw out its pastoral implications.[10] While we can point to each of these as separate statements, they are in fact essentially connected, sharing as they do the common root of the articulated vision.

1. *The call for renewed attention to adult faith formation is not primarily about establishing new programs but about gaining a new perspective on the life of the parish.*

While freeing the leadership from the immediate task of defining and implementing yet another program, this presumption points to the more challenging task of becoming a learning community.[11] It is in the context of a learning community that people continue to grow in their faith and that the ability to be an evangelizing community is enhanced.

A learning community means that learning is taking place at all levels of the parish—individuals, members of committees or groups of ministers, and the community as a whole. The task of leadership is not to generate more programs but to contribute to an environment that supports the learning of all. Unless each person within a parish is committed to learning, no program of adult formation for parish or committees will really work.

A learning community provides the space and setting in which critical reflection can take place. This involves a level of engagement with our experiences that goes beyond automatic processing to a genuine reflection on what is happening, on why it is happening, and on the implications for the future being created in the present. The process of critical reflection is complex and multilayered.[12] It is not often supported by a fast-paced culture in which everything is presented in sound bites and bulleted lists. Leadership within a learning community invites and indeed challenges all its members to engage in this at times difficult activity by working to establish an environment that allows for quiet reflection and critical conversation.

2. *Learning takes place not simply under the auspices of religious education; learning takes place in the very life and rhythm of the parish.*

All elements of the life of the parish have the potential to invite people into critical reflection. One of the core tenets of a learning community is recognition of the essential interconnection of the various elements of parish life. In discussing the nature of learning, Hawkins writes:

> Learning is comprehensive because everything the church does offers an opportunity for people to name their experiences, to recognize their assumptive frameworks and to make choices about what they know and how they know it. Teaching and learning are not limited to a single church subsystem called religious education.[13]

The more clearly we recognize and embrace the multiple ways in which people and communities grow in faith, the more effective our work will be.

But it is more than simply a pragmatic issue. The separation of catechesis from other elements of parish life—liturgy, social justice, school, and youth ministry—is simply untenable in this context. The *General Directory for Catechesis* makes clear that the cooperation and coordination of ministries of faith formation is not simply for efficiency, but is itself a witness of the call for unity and has an effect on the Church's ability to evangelize.[14]

Recognizing and fostering the fundamental interconnection of all the ways in which adults, youth, and children grow in their faith is an essential presumption for giving life to the vision of catechesis set out here.

3. *Learning as transformation is at the heart of the adult faith formation enterprise.*

At the heart of adult learning is transformative learning. As Mezirow makes clear, transformative learning involves looking closely at what we believe and think and feel in order to critically examine the assumptions that guide us. Transformative learning involves us in critical reflection not only on our experiences but also on the presumptions that shape the way in which we interpret and understand these experiences.[15]

A meeting of catechists may have as its focus the faith development of children and youth. A clear presentation contributes to the participants' knowledge of the tradition (information) and connection with the beliefs of the wider community (formation). There might even be a conversation among the catechists that explores the implications of this for how and what the catechists teach. But unless there is some means by which the adults are invited to examine their own beliefs, to gain insight into why they hold those beliefs, and to recognize the connection between this teaching and their lives as Christians, then this meeting of adults does not reflect this core presumption.

4. *Adults learn best when they are in conversation with other adults about things that matter.*

Sustained, critical conversation is at the heart of adult learning because it is essential for transformative learning.[16] At a fundamental level, I believe that providing adults with the opportunity to be in extended conversation about that which is of real consequence to them is the single most important contributor to effective and transformative learning.

Two key elements are needed for sustained critical conversation: effective questions and sufficient time. One of the most challenging aspects of facilitating good, critical conversation is finding the questions that will invite participants into the multi-layer conversation—conversation with their own presumptions, memories, and experiences, conversation with the tradition, conversation with other believers, and conversation with the future. The questions must invite participants into the exploration of the intersection of faith and life: faith and their lives, and the lives of their families and friends. That intersection is the focus of all of those multiple layers of conversation within the context of adult faith formation. While there is a tendency to gravitate to ecclesiocentric questions, the lines of inquiry that open up that intersection and invite people in are those that engage the experience of God's presence in their day-to-day lives. Instead of "What is your clearest memory of the sacrament of Reconciliation?" let me propose, "Reflect on a time of gracious forgiveness: either a time you forgave someone when it was really difficult to forgive or a time you were forgiven when you weren't really sure you were going to be. What feelings or thoughts were (or are) part of that experience for you? After taking time to remember that experience of gracious forgiveness, name one or two insights into the nature of forgiveness that you glean from this memory." Or rather than beginning the lector workshop with, "What characteristics does an effective lector need to possess?" we could begin with, "Who has been the best storyteller in your life? Tell us about that person and what made him or her such a great teller of stories." Clearly these types of questions take longer to compose and longer to answer. But they are designed to open up the conversation that brings life and faith into dialog.

The second essential element for effective sustained, critical conversation is sufficient time. Too often the "discussion time" gets shortened if or when a program starts late or a presenter goes on longer than expected. No strict formula of time distribution is going to guarantee effective adult formation or sustained conversation; however, it seems helpful to propose an overall division of one-third prayer and reflection, one-third presentation, and one-third conversation among participants. While no one session might reflect this time distribution, this can be helpfully applied to the program as a whole (e.g., the multiple meetings one has with parents involved in sacramental formation, the gathering of catechists over the course of a year). In whatever way it is facilitated, making a substantial time commitment to conversation is essential.

5. *Effective faith formation takes place in a just and hospitable space where the wisdom of all the participants is recognized and affirmed.*

Catechetical theorists like Jack Seymour, Parker Palmer, and Mary Elizabeth Moore speak of the need to create hospitable spaces where we are welcomed and heard. The term space is used in both a literal and metaphorical sense.

In speaking about adult faith formation, the hospitality of the literal space is reflected in the comfort of the surroundings, and the care given to the environment. The arrangement of the chairs serves as an important signal to the "feel" of the space and the kind of interactions that it will support. The open area within a circle of chairs speaks to the place where the thoughts and ideas of the participants can meet and mix and be received and challenged. No such open area exists in a room with rows of chairs arranged facing the podium. In addition, the presence of works of art, plants, beautiful fabric and so forth, speaks volumes for the respect that the catechist has for the participants: It is saying that you and our time together are worth the effort. Being invited into a space that has been arranged with care is an invitation into hospitality.

Speaking metaphorically, a hospitable space is marked by a spirit of mutual respect and trust. Palmer writes: "Hospitality means receiving each other, our struggles, our newborn ideas with openness and care."[17] A hospitable space is a context in which listening and speaking are both seen as active and demanding elements of conversation.[18]

While physically comfortable, aesthetically pleasing, and psychologically safe, a hospitable space doesn't mean that the learning that takes place there is comfortable and pleasing. Just the opposite, in fact. The hospitality of the learning space is essential in order that the difficult and sometimes painful work of learning can take place. Palmer articulates the point in this way:

> Hospitality is not an end in itself. It is offered for the sake of what it can allow, permit, encourage, and yield. A learning space needs to be hospitable not to make learning painless but to make the painful things possible, things without which no learning can occur—things like exposing ignorance, testing tentative hypotheses, challenging false or partial information, and mutual criticism of thought. Each of these is essential to obedience to truth. But none of them can happen in an atmosphere where people feel threatened and judged.[19]

Developing this concept of hospitality, Seymour argues that a hospitable space is also a just space, "because it honors the whole presence of each one standing in an intersection."[20] In establishing a hospitable space, the educator makes every effort to acknowledge the influence of power, to attend to the voices of the marginalized, and to recognize and affirm differences of perspective. In doing this, all who are present (and at some level even those who are absent) are recognized and respected—this is at the heart of justice.

Learning communities thrive when the insights, perspectives, and experiences of a broad base of the community are accessed and respected. A spirit of mutuality and collaboration serves as the foundation for this. The community gathers, not divided between "those in the know" and "the folks in the pew," but as people who are journeying together toward becoming a more effective evangelizing force. The wisdom of all of the members is essential.

Living into the Named Presumptions

While there are certainly other presumptions that would be worth examining as expressions of the vision named above, and there are certainly other ways to articulate the presumptions I have proposed, this discussion serves as an example of the relationship between vision and presumption. But even when they are named, the process of living into them and embracing the ramifications of the presumptions in a particular setting takes time and openness. Once a parish moves from presumptions to structures and then to program, the work continues as the program is tweaked, the structures are enhanced, and the presumptions are mined for the ongoing challenge they give to the life of the faith community.

FOR YOUR
REFLECTION AND CONVERSATION

1. In reflecting on the themes examined in the first four chapters of the book, list the central elements that you would want to integrate into a statement of vision for the catechetical work of your parish. In what ways does that complement or challenge the vision (either explicit or tacit) that guides the present model?

2. In thinking of the pairing of renewal with reform as the movement from vision to presumptions to structures to programs, what insight do you gain into the process of creating a new faith formation paradigm? In light of your own experience, what strengths do you bring to this process? What

strengths are present within the parish community? In what way is this a challenging process for you? for your parish?

3. Name a commitment or conviction that this chapter has called forth from you. What is the next step that you will take in moving toward an adult Church and an evangelizing community?

NOTES

1.   Bernard F. Swain, *Liberating Leadership: Practical Styles for Pastoral Ministry* (San Francisco: Harper & Row, 1986).

2.   Lest the ecologist among us become unduly distracted by this: I have since experienced renewal and reform and now engage in responsible recycling, and teach my daughters to do the same—thank you, Molly.

3.   NCCB, *Our Hearts Were Burning Within Us: A Pastoral Plan for Adult Faith Formation in the United States* (OHWB) (Washington, DC: USCC, 1999).

4.   Donna Markham, "Making Friends with the Dragon: Women's Leadership in a Time of Transformation," In *Human Development* 12, Summer (1991): 29.

5.   This concept is set out by Maria Harris in *Fashion Me a People: Curriculum in the Church* (Louisville, KY: Westminster/John Knox, 1989), 176–78. And in many ways that dynamic is at the heart of all creative work of faith. See, for example, the way in which this same dynamic is at the heart of the work of Jeremiah as Walter Brueggemann presents him in *The Prophetic Imagination* (Philadelphia: Fortress Press, 1978). My point is this: While the way in which vision setting and planning are described here is practically reasonable, it must also be theologically sound. As we engage in the process of planning, it is essential that it be both pragmatic and reflective of who we understand God to be, who we understand people to be, and the relationship between the two.

6.   See the following chapter for a discussion of catechist formation. As that chapter makes clear, this work of forming a community of those who serve as catechists for the parish is an essential dimension of effective catechesis at all levels but especially with adults.

7.   I am indebted to Mimi Bitzan for this image. Her role in "hosting" the parish faith formation program at St. Paul's Parish in St. Cloud, Minnesota, from 1991 to 2000 contributed in no small measure to its success.

8.   See Chapter 1 for a more detailed discussion of evangelization and its implications for how we think about the nature and mission of the Church as well as the task of catechesis.

9. Congregation for the Clergy, *General Directory for Catechesis* (*GDC*) (Washington DC: USCC, 1997).

10. I have examined some of these ideas elsewhere. See: "When Is Catechesis of Adults Genuinely Adult?" in *The Living Light* 37, no. 1 (2000).

11. This is discussed in detail in Chapter 4.

12. In discussing the centrality of critical reflection to the process of religious education, Thomas Groome articulates well its complexity. He highlights the essential interconnection of critical reasoning, critical remembering, and critical imagining. He makes clear that there is both a personal and social dimension to these. That is, in critical reasoning I not only ask questions concerning why I think or respond or understand something the way I do. I also reflect on the social realities that support this perspective. Groome makes clear that it is important to take into account this complexity and recognize that many people will be unaccustomed to engaging in this type of reflection. It seems to me important to recognize that preparing catechists and parish leadership to foster and encourage this type of reflection is also a daunting task. (See Thomas H. Groome, *Sharing Faith: A Comprehensive Approach to Religious Education and Pastoral Ministry: The Way of Shared Praxis* (San Francisco: HarperSanFrancisco, 1991), 198–208.

13. Thomas R. Hawkins, *The Learning Congregation: A New Vision of Leadership* (Louisville, KY: Westminster/John Knox, 1997), 40.

14. "The coordination of catechesis is not merely a strategic factor, aimed at more effective evangelization, but has a profound theological meaning. Evangelizing activity must be well coordinated because it touches on the *unity of faith*, which sustains all the Church's action" (*GDC* 272).

15. This concept of the centrality of transformative learning to adult education in general and adult faith formation in particular is discussed in detail in Chapter 3. The clearest overviews to the fundamental elements of Mezirow's theory can be found in "How Critical Reflection Triggers Transformative Learning," in *Fostering Critical Reflection in Adulthood* (San Francisco: Jossey-Bass, 1990). "Transformation Theory of Adult Learning," in *In Defense of the Lifeworld: Critical Perspectives on Adult Learning*, ed. Michael Welton (Albany: State University of New York Press, 1995).

16. See Chapter 4 for a discussion of the role of conversation within a learning community and its place in the process of transformative learning.

17. Parker J. Palmer, T*o Know as We Are Known: A Spirituality of Education* (San Francisco: Harper & Row, 1983), 74.

18. In an interesting study on introducing inclusive language into the worship experience in a seminary setting evidence was given of the necessity of having one's experience and feelings truly heard in order for change to take place. In comparing the experience of those who initiated or embraced change and those who resisted change, Coffman found that the most significant factor was whether or not they believed that they had been heard. Coffman writes: "One's feelings however strong or mild must be permitted expression and ac-

knowledgment in such a way that the persons know that they have been heard. In addition the hearing must include the possibility of having one's own position be changed, or at least enriched by new awareness; that is, the act of hearing another's feelings is not merely a perfunctory step to be 'gotten through.'" It is only after being heard and acknowledged that the person can hear and acknowledge the feelings and perspectives of others. (See P. M. Coffman, "Inclusive Language and Perspective Transformation" (paper presented at the 32d Annual Adult Education Research Conference, Norman, OK, 1991). As was explored in Chapter 4, this active listening is essential to transformative learning. I pick up that theme again in Chapter 7 in the discussion of leadership for change.

19. Palmer, *To Know as We Are Known*, 74.

20. Jack L. Seymour, Margaret Ann Crain, and Joseph Crockett, *Educating Christians: The Intersection of Meaning, Learning, and Vocation* (Nashville, TN: Abingdon, 1993), 91.

6

FORMING
CATECHISTS FOR AN
ADULT CHURCH

❖

A day-long workshop on the recently published document *Our Hearts Were Burning Within Us* set the call for adult faith formation within the context of the mission of the Church: Everything we do is in some way oriented to evangelization and furthering the reign of God. As the workshop continued, the participants—mostly parish catechetical leaders—were invited to name what they saw as the most challenging force working against the implementation of the document's vision for adult faith formation. While reluctant pastors, recalcitrant parish councils, and the reality of their own overextended work commitments were on the list, the comments returned again and again to issues related to the catechists. As the conversation continued, the variety of concerns clustered around two themes. The first was expressed by one of the participants in this way: "The catechists who work with the K–6 program are really pretty good. Most of them are conscientious, I think, about going over the catechist guide in advance and coming in prepared to some degree anyway. But their focus is often quite limited just to the immediate content of the session. They seldom see themselves as part of a larger activity and certainly don't see themselves within the broader context of evangelization. How do we go about broadening that?"

The second theme concerns those who work with adults and can be expressed this way: "While it is all well and good to speak about the importance of adult faith formation and the centrality of that endeavor for the life of the Church, who do we think is going to do this? Most parishes have few people with experience in adult education; many catechists and catechetical leaders simply take the presumptions and approaches that may have been well honed in their work with children or youth and simply apply them to adults. Where are we going to get the leadership who can engage in genuine adult formation?"

Without being overly simplistic, I believe that the primary response to these concerns is rooted in the way in which catechist formation takes place. If the meetings of the K–6 catechists attend primarily to the process and details of keeping the program moving smoothly—discussing the logistics of an upcoming liturgical event, outlining the lessons that need to be covered over the next several weeks, and strategizing on how best to engage the multiple learning styles of the children, the results will be catechists who attend primarily to the process and content of their part of the program with little motivation or encouragement to see the larger picture. And if the process of catechist formation and the formation of other ministers within the parish is lax in incorporating principles of adult education and transformative learning, it should be of little surprise that the catechists of adults follow the lead of "teaching as they were taught" and neglect to attend to the genuinely *adult* nature of adult faith formation. My conviction is that catechists and others engaged in the catechetical enterprise cannot give expression to what they have not experienced.

Before continuing, I invite you to pause for a moment and reflect on your experience of catechist formation either as a catechist or a catechetical leader who plans and facilitates the process. Here are some questions to guide your reflection and conversation:

1. If someone from the outside were to analyze the various forms of catechist formation that take place in the course of a year, what conclusion might he or she draw about the goal or focus of such formation?

2. If the formation process of a given year were divided into a time pie using these categories—Prayer and Reflection, Presentation, Structured Conversation, and Other—what would it look like?

3. If someone from the outside were to look at the catechist formation process as an example of adult education, what principles, or presumptions about the nature of adult learning, might he or she draw from that experience?

An examination of two themes defines the flow of this chapter. The first is in response to the question What are the elements of formation that are essential to the ministry of catechist formation? And the second answers the question How do we engage in catechist formation in such a way as to engage the imaginative and transformative learning of the participants? In responding to these questions, a proposal for catechist formation emerges that both forms people for the specific ministry of catechist, and invites them to be participants of an adult, evangelizing community.

FORMATION: DEVELOPMENTAL AND ARTISTIC

In beginning this discussion of catechist formation, some attention to the term *formation* is warranted. The word itself suggests both a developmental and an artistic connotation.[1] On the one hand, to speak of formation is to refer to the way in which it develops or grows over time and the process by which that development is supported. The term *formation* also suggests that one's growth occurs across a variety of dimensions: physical, psychological, spiritual, intellectual. Each of these can be used to modify the term *development* and are among the aspects that we might include when we consider what it means "to form disciples" or "to be formed by a community's life and values."

But we can also note that formation suggests an artistic dimension, for "to form" or "to give form" refers us to the artist. The sculptor, for example, helps to give shape to that which is already there, that which is undefined, raw, and open to the process of being formed. The developmental dimension of formation places an emphasis on accruing more insight and becoming more sophisticated in how one interprets the world; it points to a relatively smooth growth over time. This artistic dimension of formation evokes a more intense and often circuitous route. It speaks not so much of a moving forward but of a breaking out and an uncovering.

A theorist who has drawn on this sense of formation in discussing the process of religious education is Maria Harris. In the opening chapters of *Fashion Me a People: Curriculum in the Church*, Harris works with the assorted derivatives of *form*, much as an artist works with clay, to disclose the ways in which the dynamics of education can be perceived as the "fashioning and refashioning of the forms that human life offers, the forms we shape as artists at the same time we allow those forms to shape us."[2] Harris proposes that religious education involves taking the forms of Church life—teaching, proclamation, service, liturgy, and community—and lifting them up as forms through which we are transformed. Catechesis involves us in educating both to these forms and through these forms; we become more of a people of prayer by engaging in prayer, and we are formed into a people of service by engaging in service and allowing that form to transform us.

To engage in "formation" invites us to bring together these two complementary perspectives: the developmental, with its emphasis on the accruing of more insight, more information, even, and the artistic, with its recognition that formation is about embracing our experiences as people of faith and allowing them to form and transform us. At the point of intersection of these perspectives, we find an understanding of formation that is holistic, interdisciplinary, and multifaceted. We recognize it as a complex enterprise that brings into play the many ways in which the catechist is called to engage in the process of catechesis.

The approach that the *General Directory for Catechesis (GDC)* uses in speaking about catechist[3] formation provides a helpful resource for bringing the two dimensions of formation together. The chapter "Formation for the Service of Catechists" attends with care and detail to the importance of the basic training and ongoing formation of catechists at every level. The writers of the *GDC* make clear the importance of catechist formation: "The instruments provided for catechesis cannot be truly effective unless well used by trained catechists. Thus the adequate *formation of catechists* cannot be overlooked by concerns such as the updating of texts or the reorganization of catechesis" (234). They go on to assert that catechist formation must be attentive to the broader task of catechesis, that is the overall vision of the catechetical enterprise.

Five "inspiring" criteria of the formation of catechists are listed: (1) The formation of catechists is rooted in the call to evangelization and supports catechists in their sense of faith, their ecclesial identity, and their social sensitivity. (2) It emphasizes the essential connection between instruction and formation. (3) It assists catechists in their ability to articulate Church teaching in an inclusive and evocative way. (4) It recognizes the distinctive contribution of the laity and sets this out as an essential contribution of lay catechists. (5) It follows a pedagogical style that is in keeping with the appropriate pedagogy of catechesis (*GDC* 237). In enumerating these, the writers of the *GDC* make clear the essential connection between the aims and means of catechesis and the aims and means of catechist formation. There is to be a clear connection between the understanding of catechesis and the way catechist formation is planned, structured, and implemented.

In light of this conversation, the dimensions of formation are set out: "being, knowing, and savoir-faire." Let me propose here that the significance of these three elements is not simply that they are areas that need to be addressed in the formation of catechists. They are significant because they point to the very essence of the work of the catechist: the catechist engages in this ministry as person of faith, theologian, and educator. To be a catechist is to draw on who one is, what one believes, and how one engages with others . . . being, knowing, and savoir-faire.

Catechist as Person of Faith: Being

The writers of the *GDC* make clear, and I concur, that the most significant dimension relates to the catechist as person of faith. They write: "The deepest dimension refers to the very being of the catechist, to his [and her] human and Christian dimension. Formation, above all else, must help him [and her] to mature as a person, a believer and as an apostle" (*GDC* 238). Ultimately, it is as a person of faith that we are most effective in our ministry as catechist.

Undergraduate students in a required introductory theology class provide an interesting lens to the catechetical work of the Church. I have taught introductory theology courses in four different settings since 1983, and each time I have taught it, I have asked the students to write a short essay that highlights the experiences that have had a positive influence on their engagement with God or Church or faith as well as those experiences which have had a negative influence. Although the discussion of negative influences has varied, the descriptions of positive influences share many similarities: in almost all cases, the students make reference to some person (at this age, usually not their parents) whose lived faith had a significant impact on the student's sense of God or Church or what it means to be a believer. While this might have been a catechist or a youth minister, a coach or a teacher, it was seldom *what* they said that influenced the young person; it was *who* they were as people of faith.

One of the stories points clearly to the centrality of the lived faith of those who enhanced the faith life of the young person. It was recounted by a sophomore who wrote about an experience that had happened a few years earlier. For reasons that were not clear in the essay, the student had plagiarized a major paper at the conclusion of her theology class at the end of her junior year in high school. She "borrowed" a paper from a friend who had written it for another teacher a couple of years earlier. The student got caught and the repercussions were significant. But what she remembered most clearly about the event was the compassion and respect with which the theology teacher treated her. In telling the story, the student makes clear that her theology teacher, rooted in her love for the students and her love of her field, was able to challenge this young woman to rethink her priorities and to look into the gifts and abilities that she has. She certainly learned her lesson, one part of which was not to plagiarize! But she learned another lesson as well: She saw modeled in her theology teacher a person of faith who by her actions reflected God's love and forgiveness. It is of little surprise that the student decided to major in secondary education and theology. In reflecting on this account and similar ones received over the years, a connection can be drawn to the concept of "vocation." James Fowler describes vocation in these terms:

> . . . the response a person makes with his or her total self to the address of God and to the calling to partnership. The shaping of vocation as total response of the self to the address

of God involves the orchestration of our leisure, our relationships, our work and private life, our public life, and of the resources we steward, so as to put it all at the disposal of God's purpose in the services of God and the neighbor.[4]

Fowler makes clear that vocation is not to a job or career but to a way of being in the world that is a response to the address of God, to the invitation of partnership with God. This call to partnership permeates all the actions and decisions that a person makes in a day, in a year, in a lifetime.[5] It is in being grounded in this vocation that the catechist is able to live into a sense of her identity and integrity as a person of faith.

Parker Palmer uses those terms—*identity* and *integrity*—in the opening chapter of *The Courage to Teach*. He writes of the interrelationship of identity and integrity and the importance of these elements to an effective teacher. Identity can be understood as the coming together of all of the elements of our lives, as the wholeness of who we are in the variety of settings. Identity, Palmer writes, "is a moving intersection of the inner and outer forces that make me who I am, converging in the irreducible mystery of being human."[6] Recognizing the multiple dimensions of who we are and working to keep those in healthful relationship while negotiating the busy intersections of our lives are at the heart of integrity. "*Identity* lies in the intersection of the diverse forces that make up my life, and *integrity* lies in relating to those forces in ways that bring me wholeness and life rather than fragmentation and death."[7] In ways that connect with Fowler's notion of vocation as an "orchestration" of all that we have, living in integrity involves acknowledging what is the essence of selfhood, and being aware of harmonizing these dimensions in a life-giving way.[8] Palmer proposes that good teaching is not simply about technique; good teaching takes place when it is rooted in the identity and integrity of the teacher.

What does this mean for the catechist and the way we approach catechist formation? The end of this chapter includes some proposed guidelines for how one plans and implements an integrated process of catechist formation; a few preliminary points can be made here.

At a fundamental level, effective catechist formation begins with the way in which people are invited into the ministry of catechesis. The regular appearance in the Sunday bulletin of the statement "Fifth and sixth grade catechists needed" belies the reality that there is a charism inherent to the work of catechesis and that the gift is not given to everyone. Just as those who are part of the parish's music ministry—whether cantor or musician or choir member—are expected to give evidence of the appropriate musical gifts and talents; just as members of the parish council are recognized by community members as having gifts of leadership: those who are catechists are called forth and recognized because of their gifts. Whether we are thinking of those working with adults or with youth and children, our fundamental sense is that the catechist is one whose faith is clearly expressed and most powerfully fostered in the act of catechesis. In the best expression of this ministry, catechists engage in their ministry not only as a service to the faith community and to the adults or children with whom they work; they are catechists because it is there that their own faith is fostered.

Donna has served as director and primary catechist of the RCIA process in her parish for the past four years. It is a time-consuming task. In talking about her experience, Donna affirms that her ministry as a catechist has been one of the most important means by which her own faith has been fostered. "I love Lent!" she states. "There is something about the intensity with which we study the readings. And the rhythm of prayer and study and ritual. . . . By the time the Triduum comes I am ready to hear again the defining stories of our faith tradition and reaffirm my place in the Christian community." Donna serves in the ministry of the RCIA not only to be of service to the catechumens, candidates, and their sponsors; she serves because it is there that her own faith is fostered.

How different to replace the bulletin announcement "Sixth grade catechist for Monday afternoon classes still needed. Call for more information." with "Invitation to those whose own faith is fostered by sharing it with children and youth and other adults. Come share your gifts and faith with us!" In the context of Palmer's understanding of teaching, a catechist is one whose identity comes to expression in the role of catechist and whose sense of integrity is enhanced by that ministry. Attending to the "being" dimension of the catechist begins with the way in which we invite people to the work.

Part of the invitation also includes a sincere and honest appraisal of the commitment that is being asked for. The tendency to minimize the time, energy, and spirit that are essential to being an effective catechist leads to disappointing results all around: The director or coordinator of religious education is frustrated at the lack of participation in catechists' meetings; the catechist is overwhelmed by her lack of success in the sessions and her feeling of never being quite ready; and every year a new set of catechists has to be found because the turnover rate is so high. It is more effective and engaging to invite catechists into a community of people who gather from time to time for prayer and community, who share in the common mission of catechesis, and whose faith is enriched by the interaction among the catechists and by the engagement with adults, children, or youth in the catechetical enterprise. The catechist formation process should then embody these opportunities.

Catechist as Theologian: "Knowing"

The second dimension of catechist formation is that of "knowing." The writers of the *GDC* set this out as a knowing that is connected to the catechist's commitment to the Christian message and to the human beings involved. The catechist is to have "sufficient knowledge of the message," as well as of those with whom she or he shares the message and "the social context in which they live" (*GDC* 238). So, catechists are called to know the message and know the people.

As we look at how to integrate this dimension of knowing into the process of catechist formation, two elements seem to be important. First is the conviction that all Christian knowing is for Christian living. For the believer, the Christian story is never simply interesting information; the work of the catechist can never end with the effective transmission of the facts of the Christian story. The knowing must be situated in the *context* of the lives of the learners and support an ever deepening commitment to Jesus Christ expressed in lived Christian faith.

One spring, on the Friday before Holy Week, I was picking up my younger daughter from school (she was in kindergarten at the time). As she got into the car she informed me: "I know what this Sunday is." "Really," I responded. "What is it?" "It's Pompom Sunday!" she replied, quite proud of herself. "Do you mean *Palm* Sunday?" I asked. And with the look that a six year old can give her parent when she is amazed at how little the parent knows, Catie replied: "No, it's Pompom Sunday! Everybody is saying 'Hosanna' and cheering for Jesus and waving their pompoms! We need pompoms to cheer for somebody." She had been to enough college football games to know how to cheer. And that does put a new image on Jesus' triumphal entry into Jerusalem! I was right, as I *knew* it was Palm Sunday; but she was right because she *knew* what it means to cheer for Jesus.

On the one hand, the "knowing" that is essential to the work of the catechist is a knowing that keeps at the center the link between faith and life. and It is not simply about information but formation and transformation as well.[9] At the same time, the catechist is called to a "knowing" of Church teaching that is coherent, systematic, and balanced. In some ways, Palmer's notion of identity and integrity can be applied in a broad sense to how a catechist is to approach the Christian tradition. For Palmer, identity and integrity are about keeping in positive relationship the total experience of our lives—our past, present, and future—and seeing the wholeness as a synthesis of who we are and what serves as a genuine expression of selfhood. It is knowing who we are and who we are becoming in light of who we have been, that serves as the sure grounding for the work of teaching. In a similar way, the catechist's knowing of the Christian tradition requires a similar relationship between past and future. It requires a balance of memory and openness.[10]

As a Church we are rooted in a long and solid tradition—we are a Church that recognizes and affirms a wide range of thinkers and scholars, hermits and mystics. They represent a diverse collection of women and men, sinners and saints, academically formed and self-educated. Particularly in the years following Vatican Council II, those whose ideas, insights, and experiences serve as the foundation of the Christian tradition and the Church's teaching represent a growing diversity of ethnic, cultural, and national backgrounds. So when catechists today come to any specific teaching—the humanity and divinity of Jesus, the nature of the Church, an understanding of sacraments, ways of reading Scripture, the elements of Catholic social teaching—they join a large and lively conversation that has been taking place within the Christian community for 2000 years, and that is in continuity with a still longer conversation that we trace back to the call of Abraham. As today's catechists attempt to "know" the Christian tradition in a way that is accessible to them and their students, they do this not only with the insights of today's Church but with a sense of respect for the way in which the Church has given expression to it in the past. We are a people who are rooted in the firm foundation of the past, a people who value and depend on *memory*.

On the other hand, the Church exists not as a past, complete, static reality but as a living, breathing entity located in history, expected to speak in a way that addresses present reality. In addition to memory that holds firmly to the past, we need openness that allows us to move into the future. As we look at the Church in the present and into the future, we recognize that there are new questions, new experiences, new perspectives that the Church has never had to address. While memory provides an essential framework for responding, without openness to the experience and insights of believers today, that memory runs the risk of being static and sterile.

The challenge is to maintain the balance: Openness without memory leads to a kind of faddishness and a relativity that says that all directions into the future are the same. It is interesting to think about the significant times in the history of the Church as those times in which there was a struggle to sustain the balance between memory and openness. Memory without openness becomes dry and static, a calcified remembrance of a once living church. The balance of memory and openness is at the core of the catechist's "knowing" the Christian message in a way that has the power to transform. Only then can the catechist proclaim it as the transforming Good News for others.

The *GDC* makes clear that it is not simply knowledge of the Church's teachings that suffices when speaking about the "knowing" that is necessary for catechists. The second "knowing" that is central to catechist formation is related to how the catechists understand the learners and their social and cultural contexts. There are multiple dimensions to this discussion of knowing the learner: the social-psychological, where the work of Erik Erikson is so crucial;[11] developmental theorists who build on the thoughts of Jean Piaget;[12] and those who specifically look at faith development with James Fowler as a central voice.[13] In addition, issues of learning style and an awareness of "multiple intelligences" are also important in how we know the learner.[14] A secondary dimension is a cultural one[15]—how does the perspective of the Baby Boomers, the Gen-X'ers or the Millennium Generation shape the way in which the Gospel is proclaimed? What are the characteristics of the postmodern culture within which catechesis takes place, shapes and forms the cate-chist as a person of faith and as theologian? When we speak about "knowing," it includes knowing the learners as well.

We return to the question of the implications of this dis-cussion for catechist formation. Some guidelines are examined at the end of this chapter, but two themes seem particularly per-tinent to this focus on "knowing."

First, in exploring the way in which the catechist is called to *know the learner*, fostering the awareness of the catechist's own social and moral development is important. Recognizing that teachers often teach to their own dominant style of learning, raising the awareness on the part of each catechist of how he or she learns best and the variety of ways in which other people learn is helpful.[16] Most important, providing a context where the catechists can reflect on their own faith and the way in which it was fostered when they were children, youth, and now as adults is essential to effective catechist formation.

Second, in supporting the catechist in responding to the call to *know the Church's teaching*, the Christian message is presented in a style that moves beyond information and invites the cate-chist into commitment and conversion. Simply taking a theol-ogy course at the local Catholic college does not necessarily suffice for the type of theological foundation that the catechist needs.[17] A model of theological reflection provides an effective approach to enhancing the catechist's theological understand-ing in a way that will enhance his or her ability to express the Christian message in life and in teaching. In theological reflec-tion the experience of the participants serves as an essential ele-ment of the manifestation of God's presence among us. The Christian tradition is understood and appreciated in its ability to illumine, clarify, challenge, and make more accessible these experiences as experiences of God.[18]

What becomes clear from this discussion is that the cate-chist's growing knowledge of the faith is rooted in the dynamic relationship between content and process. They cannot be separated. It is specious to propose that the Catholic tradition can be conveyed without carefully thinking about the approach used, or to think that a catechist formation process can spend a certain number of sessions on content and then move on to process. The way in which the Christian message is taught has an impact on both how the catechist comes to understand Church teaching *and* how he or she engages others in coming to new insight about the Christian message and the implications for lived Christian faith.[19] Thus, we turn to the third essential element of catechist formation: savoir-faire.

Catechist as Educator: Savoir-faire

Here the writers of the *GDC* point to the importance of cultivating catechists' "know-how," but this is more than simply teaching a series of effective techniques. The point of intersection between knowing the learner and knowing the Christian story is where the catechist brings into play the skills that allow catechesis to form, inform, and transform. The *GDC* includes the statement: "Formation seeks to mature an education capacity in the catechist which implies: an ability to be attentive to people, an ability to interpret or respond to educational tasks or initiatives in organizing learning activities and the ability of leading a human group toward maturity" (*GDC* 244). Savoir-faire is not about technique in a narrow sense but is a way of talking about the perspective or attitude as well as the ability of the catechist to engage others in conversation about issues of faith: a conversation that is essential for the move toward maturity of faith.

To bring this discussion of savoir-faire to conclusion, three observations are helpful. First, our volunteer catechists do need information in both dimensions of "know-how": knowing the tradition and knowing the learners. Essential are conversations around contemporary notions of ecclesiology, Christology, sacramental theology, and moral theology, as well as Christian anthropology, faith development theory, and fundamental education theory. For example, many of the catechists with whom we work have not had the opportunity to step back to reflect on the anthropology and the understanding of revelation inherent to the catechetical process most series use, which begins with the experience of the learners. Too many catechists do not understand that we connect with the experience of the learners not simply to get their attention or to name issues in their lives where the teaching of the session may apply; we connect with the experience of the learners because we believe that in that experience, God is present and revealed. Explicit formation in this area is important.

Second, in addition to sessions that examine this type of content, it is also essential that new catechists be connected with more experienced and reflective catechists who can serve as mentors. Establishing that relationship gives the new catechist a context for exploring her understanding of the catechetical ministry and her place within it. In addition, the mentoring relationship serves to encourage both parties to be more reflective about their teaching; it provides both with a setting for talking about their own spiritual growth.[20] While the information given to catechists in meetings or in the catechist guide can be helpful and necessary, at the heart of forming effective catechists is the process of learning by doing with reflection and self-evaluation.

Finally, reiterating a point that was made earlier: All catechist formation must be reflective of the core principles of adult catechesis. If the invitation to be a catechist is issued in the terms used above—"Invitation to those whose own faith is fostered by sharing it with children and youth and other adults. Come share your gifts and faith with us!"—then it is incumbent upon the leadership to be sure that the catechist formation engages the faith growth of those involved. A brief examination of the presumptions that I set out in Chapter 5 as implications for catechist formation is helpful.

CATECHIST FORMATION AS
ADULT CATECHESIS

1. *The call for renewed attention to adult faith formation is
   not primarily about establishing new programs but about
   gaining a new perspective on the life of the parish.*

The invitation in this chapter is not necessarily to do more
in the way of catechist formation but to take a perspective on
the process that fosters the real growth in faith of the catechists
within the parish community. It might be helpful to begin by
giving some expression to what you understand the vision and
presumptions of the parish process of catechist formation are
and what they could be.

Catechist formation shares in the overall movement of catechesis, which has as its focus and charge the formation of an
evangelizing community. In many ways the catechists are invited
to serve as a central core around which other parts of the parish
community connect with the evangelizing work. So the process
of forming catechists is first and foremost to form them into an
evangelizing community.

The concern raised by the DREs at the opening of this
chapter is an important one: how do catechetical leaders energize catechists to see their role and their ministry as part of
the larger reality of the Church's mission? To a large degree,
the focus and approach to catechist formation serve to define
the range of interest of those involved in catechesis. Being intentional about setting the role of the catechist in the wider
work of evangelization and seeing catechist formation as formation in service to the mission of the Church and not merely
to Church membership are essential to engaging catechists in
the wider endeavor.

What impact does it have on the way in which you think of
catechist formation if you look at it through the lens of the call
to evangelization?

2. *Learning takes place not simply under the auspices of religious education; learning takes place in the very life and rhythm of the parish.*

This presumption, when applied to the work of catechist formation, urges the catechetical leader to look beyond the specifics of a program that he or she may have planned to all of the ways in which the catechists grow in their understanding of the Christian tradition and their commitment of faith. Recognizing and fostering the fundamental interconnection of all the ways in which catechists grow in their faith is an essential presumption for giving life to the vision of catechesis set out here.

In what ways is catechist formation set within the context of the wider parish and all the ways in which parish ministers and all adults are invited to grow in their faith and their understanding of ministry?

3. *Learning as transformation is at the heart of the adult faith formation enterprise.*

With this presumption applied to the work of catechist formation, we move off of a strictly instrumental learning—learning what I need to know to fulfill the job of the catechist—to transformative learning, which involves us in critical reflection not only on our experiences but on the presumptions that shape the way in which we interpret and understand these experiences. While the focus and goal of a particular gathering of catechists may be quite specifically addressed to the smooth operation of the program, how do we do this in such a way as to invite the ongoing transformation of the catechist as a person of faith?

4. *Adults learn best when they are in conversation with other adults about things that matter.*

The two elements that are essential to fulfilling this presumption are the formation of effective, evocative questions and the structuring of sufficient time for extended conversation. It is essential to remind ourselves repeatedly that the concerns of catechist formation serve as the topic around which we are inviting this group of adults into conversation about things that matter in their lives. At times this is easier to see when we look at formation programs for sacraments. We know that the gathering of parents around themes for first Eucharist has the double focus of acquainting them with the program and inviting them into conversation with other adults. The same dynamics are at play here. While the theme of the catechist meeting may be related to a unit on the Beatitudes or to preparation for Lent, the opening questions are designed to invite the catechists into conversation with the meaning of that theme for their lives as people of faith. Unless the catechists are invited, encouraged, and challenged to reflect critically on their own presumptions and understandings of the significance of an aspect of the Christian tradition for their lives, they cannot facilitate that critical reflection in others. In fact, if they have not done their own critical reflection, they may well discourage it in others as being too challenging and intimidating a task.

In addition to asking effective questions, sustained critical conversation also requires sufficient time. The rhythm that I suggested in the previous chapter—one-third of the time for prayer and reflection, one-third for presentation, and one-third for conversation among participants seems helpful here. The tendency to be highly task oriented tends to lead to a shortening of the first and third elements and an emphasis on the presentation. And with catechist formation that often translates into a series of extended announcements.

In what ways would your model of catechist formation change if you followed the scheduling guideline of one third of the time for each activity—prayer and reflection, presentation, and conversation?

5. *Effective faith formation takes place in a just and hospitable space where the wisdom of all the participants is recognized and affirmed.*

Effective engagement in the central themes of catechist formation—being, knowing, and savoir-faire—requires a space of hospitality. The care that is given to the physical space in preparation for the gathering and to the metaphorical space as the session unfolds speaks loudly of the importance of the faith life of the catechist. And in this hospitable space, catechists are able to give expression to their faith and try out new ways of speaking about God and speaking to God.

One of my contentions concerning the reluctance of some adults to speak about their faith—either to their children or to other adults—is a lack of practice. The process of talking with others about important matters helps us to gain clarity in our own thinking and broadens the perspective that we bring to it. And so, as I stated above, conversation among catechists is essential. The point here is that conversation needs to take place in a hospitable space where the experience and insights of all are respected.

There is another important reason for attending to the space within which catechist formation takes place: it models for the catechists the care they are called to show to the adults, youth, or children with whom they minister. The sense of hospitality, welcome, safety, and justice that we want to have at the heart of the catechetical environment will only be there if our catechists experience it themselves.

In what ways might you improve the hospitality of the space within which catechist formation takes place? What would be some ways of making it more hospitable and just?

FOR YOUR
REFLECTION AND CONVERSATION

1. Review the questions raised at the beginning of the chapter. What new insights do you bring to your reflection on your present model of catechist formation?

2. Reflect on the three roles that the catechist has—as person of faith, as theologian, and as teacher. Which is most important in your experience? Which is most in need of support?

3. Name two or three ways in which you can address some of the key challenges in catechist formation in your pastoral setting.

NOTES

1.   I am grateful to Michael Horan for pointing out these two ways of thinking about the term *formation*. We examined this in a nascent way in the address entitled "The Direction of Catechetical Leadership in the New Millennium" that we gave to the National Conference of Catechetical Leadership, April 19, 1999, in Indianapolis.

2.   Maria Harris, *Fashion Me a People: Curriculum in the Church* (Louisville, KY: Westminster/John Knox, 1989), 41.

3.   When international ecclesial documents, such as the *GDC* or "Adult Catechesis in the Christian Community," use the term catechists, they are usually referring to people responsible for a core element of the larger catechetical work. In many places in the United States, this may correspond more closely to catechetical leaders: those who work full time as DREs or parish coordinators or those who work part-time as directors of the RCIA or catechetical leaders for sacramental formation. However, while some of the issues discussed in the *GDC* may have application primarily to the full-time DRE and to others in leadership, many of the themes and points of formation apply to the facilitator of an adult faith-sharing group or the catechist of the third-grade peer group.

4.   James W. Fowler, *Becoming Adult, Becoming Christian: Adult Development and Christian Faith* (San Francisco: Harper & Row, 1984), 95.

5.   It seems to me that this sense of vocation also points us back to the discussion on apprenticeship as a way to speak about the Christian journey and the work of catechesis. See the discussion of apprenticeship in Chapter 1.

6.   Parker J. Palmer, *The Courage to Teach: Exploring the Inner Landscape of a Teacher's Life* (San Francisco: Jossey-Bass, 1998), 13.

7.   Ibid.

8. This also connects with Erikson's understanding of identity and particularly the adolescent's engagement with the tension between identity and identity confusion. For Erikson, the central task for the adolescent and for the ongoing work of forming one's identity is to look back on one's past and ask "What do I have?" and look to the future to ask "What am I going to do with what I have?"

9. See Chapter 1 for a more detailed discussion of the dynamics of catechesis and the essential connection among the elements of formation, information, and transformation.

10. This idea of the fundamental relationship between memory and openness is articulated well by Lawrence Cunningham in *The Catholic Experience* (New York: Crossroads, 1985). See particularly the chapter "Catholicity."

11. The contribution of Erikson is discussed in some detail in Chapter 2. For an overview of Erikson's theory, the best resource is Erik Erikson, *The Life Cycle Completed, Extended Version with New Chapters on the Ninth Stage of Development by Joan M. Erikson* (New York: Norton, 1997). A helpful commentary that provides a solid and engaging introduction to Erikson's theory is Francis L. Gross, *Introducing Erik Erikson: An Invitation to His Thinking* (Lanham, MD: University Press of America, 1987).

12. Particularly helpful in understanding the basic concepts of Piaget's schema are two books: Jean Piaget, *Six Psychological Studies* (New York: Random House, 1967), and Jean Claude Bringuier and Jean Piaget, *Conversations with Jean Piaget* (Chicago: University of Chicago Press, 1980). James Fowler includes a helpful section in his book *Stages of Faith: The Psychology of Human Development and the Quest for Meaning* (San Francisco: Harper & Row, 1981) 37–89, "Part II: Windows on Human Development: A Fictional Conversation" in which he brings into dialog the perspectives of Erikson, Piaget, and Kohlberg.

13. The key works by Fowler that examine his stages of development are James W. Fowler, Sam Keen, and Jerome Berryman, *Life Maps: Conversations on the Journey of Faith* (Waco, TX: Word Books, 1978), and Fowler, *Stages of Faith*. An important resource for a critical read on Fowler's faith development theory is Craig R. Dykstra and Sharon Parks, *Faith Development and Fowler* (Birmingham, AL: Religious Education Press, 1986).

14. The primary name connected with the foundational idea of multiple intelligences is Howard Gardner. His original explanation of multiple intelligences and the seven specific intelligences that he identified in his research can be found in his book *Frames of Mind: The Theory of Multiple Intelligences* (New York: Basic Books, 1983). His most recent book develops his core ideas and adds the eighth one, the naturalist intelligence, *Intelligence Reframed: Multiple Intelligences for the 21st Century* (New York: Basic Books, 1999).

15. It would be within the scope of what we are discussing here to set out the dynamics of contemporary culture and its implications for catechesis and for the Christian vision. A number of books examine elements of this question. Accessible, though perhaps not as clearly nuanced as some other books is

Michael Paul Gallagher, *Clashing Symbols: An Introduction to Faith and Culture* (New York: Paulist Press, 1998). Gallagher does a good job of setting out the central themes of a postmodern context. Looking at the significance of postmodernity for Christian theology is Paul Lakeland, *Postmodernity: Christian Identity in a Fragmented Age* (Minneapolis, MN: Fortress Press, 1997). Finally, Kenan B. Osborne, *Christian Sacraments in a Postmodern World: A Theology for the Third Millennium* (New York: Paulist Press, 1999), provides an analysis of the postmodern construction through the lens of sacramental theology.

16. In David A. Kolb, *Experiential Learning: Experience as the Source of Learning and Development* (Englewood Cliffs, NJ: Prentice-Hall, 1984), Kolb examines learning cycle in terms of dominant learning styles. Subsequent to his research he developed the "Learning Style Inventory," which was revised in 1985 and published by McBer and Company (http://trgmcber.haygroup.com). The inventory is designed to give people a way of recognizing their own learning type and the strengths and challenges that accompany it. It is helpful to have the catechists complete this tool in a group and then chart the diversity within the group of catechists. Discussing the types of activities that are effective for the various learning styles is important; this works to enhance the catechists' savoir-faire.

17. In several places the *GDC* makes clear that catechesis requires an understanding of Church teaching that has as its foundation the call to conversion and the intimate connection between life and faith. This is particularly clear in #241 in which the theological foundations for the catechist are examined.

18. Particularly helpful are the models set out in James D. Whitehead and Evelyn Eaton Whitehead, *Method in Ministry: Theological Reflection and Christian Ministry* (San Francisco: Harper & Row, 1980), as well as shared Christian praxis in Thomas H. Groome, *Sharing Faith: A Comprehensive Approach to Religious Education and Pastoral Ministry: The Way of Shared Praxis* (San Francisco: HarperSanFrancisco, 1991).

19. This is particularly the case when the catechists are being prepared to work with adults. Most materials for children include a good deal of discussion of the process that the catechist is to use. Often, however, the process that is set out in resources for adults does not engage the participants at the point of intersection between their present praxis and the Christian tradition.

20. A helpful resource for exploring a structured model for establishing and supporting mentors can be found in Leona M. English, *Mentoring in Religious Education* (Birmingham, AL: Religious Education Press, 1998). Drawing on a range of research from a variety of settings, English sets out the potential, dimensions, and challenges to effective mentoring. While a formal structure as defined as English proposes might not be possible or necessary for volunteer catechists, many of the insights and elements she discusses would be helpful.

7

Toward an Adult Church: Leadership for Change

❖

In his book on congregations as learning communities, Thomas Hawkins tells of a friend's first experience going white-water rafting. There were four rules that she had to learn before she could get into the water.

> First, rest in the calm spots because there are always more rapids ahead. Second, when heading for a rock, lean into the rock rather than away from it. Third, never stop paddling. Fourth, let go of everything but your life jacket if you fall into the water.[1]

Hawkins goes on to say, "These rules also apply to ministry in a permanent white-water society." A core thesis of Hawkins's book is that the rapidity of change in all aspects of our lives—a permanent white-water society—requires a new understanding of leadership and the role of the congregation as a learning community.

Certainly the pages of this book serve as an invitation and a challenge to embrace change and to facilitate a new paradigm for how we think about and engage in the work of catechesis at the parish and diocesan levels. The fundamental change in focus that is at the heart of this book—a shift from an emphasis on children and youth to a stress on the faith development of adults—requires significant openness to change. Even the words of assurance, which have often been given in this book, that this does not mean neglecting the children in favor of the adults, does not help the feeling that many may have that we are in a fairly small raft and heading for the rocks. I believe that these are exciting but potentially scary times in the life of the Church, and the place of effective leadership in navigating the depths and shoals in this white-water ride is essential.

This chapter thus serves as an invitation to reflect on issues of leadership, particularly connected to leadership in time of change. This chapter is somewhat different in approach from the others as it invites you into conversation with your past experience and your future hopes. These pages are best done in extended conversations with others who share your passion for adult faith formation and the future of the Church as an evangelizing agent in the world.

We begin by examining our experiences and reaction to change, and then we consider elements of institutional change and the reactions and resistance that often come with it. In the second section we reflect on the demands on leaders in times of change and the role that they are to play. In speaking about the insights that contributed to his description of servant leadership, Robert Greenleaf reflected on the gifts of American journalist and writer E. B. White. Greenleaf writes: "Mr. White, I soon learned, had two gifts that are seldom possessed by one person: the ability to see things whole, or more whole than most, and the language to tell us ordinary mortals what he saw."[2] It seems that this is an apt description of the gifts that a leader needs in facing and facilitating change. I invite you to reflect on that as we examine the role of leader and the experience of change.

Times of Change

We have all experienced change at various points in our lives—change that we have initiated and some that has been thrust on us by others. Whatever forces contribute the change in our lives and in our ministries, how we think about change needs to be considered. At issue in this conversation is how we perceive change. Do we see it as a threat to who we are as a Church, an institution, a society? Is the necessity for change seen as a negative evaluation of what we have been doing in the past? Or do we see it as an inevitable part of life and as an opportunity to reexamine past values and affirm present visions as they are coming to expression in the future? Reflecting on our own experience of change serves as an important beginning point.

Naming Our Experience of Change

Call to mind two or three key experiences of change: perhaps a change in leadership in your parish or work setting, perhaps a change in your focus of ministry that was introduced by you or by others, perhaps a time of change brought on by a specific crisis or opportunity.

As possible, think of times in which you have been part of the process for introducing change and times in which you have been the "recipient" of the changes others have made. Call to mind those times in which change has been effectively carried out and times in which it seemed to be more difficult than it needed to be.

After calling to mind these various experiences, reflect on these questions and engage in conversation with others.

1. What is your own reaction to change, generally speaking? What difference does your role in the process of change make in your reaction? List the characteristics of situations of change that you think have an impact on your response to change.

2. What is the role of people in leadership in effectively facilitating change? What would characterize those leaders who are good at introducing change? Presuming that all leaders hope to introduce change in ways that are effective, what do you think keeps people from effectively bringing about change?

The Reality of Change

In all aspects of our lives, change is inevitable. A way of parenting that worked last month seems ineffective today. The model of decision making in a company or business becomes a block to timely judgments rather than a help. The assignment that was so effective a couple of semesters ago no longer has the desired impact on the students' learning and understanding. The model for acquiring and training volunteer catechists that seemed to work pretty well for years is having poor results. In small ways and significant ones we are invited, challenged, or dragged into the process of change. Sometimes the change is precipitated primarily by specific outside forces and by decisions made by others. Sometimes we bring the need for change into focus ourselves through shifts in our attitudes or perceptions; new insights into a situation make it clear to us that the present model is not working as well as we had hoped. And always the necessity of change is brought about when a configuration of forces makes a mode of action that has been effective up to now no longer feasible.

One way to understand change is to take the process of change apart a bit and step back to see where we are. A helpful model for thinking about the process of change is to see it as a cyclical process of genesis, growth, stabilization, breakdown, and dis-integration, leading back to genesis.[3]

Exploring this cycle through the lens of an example is helpful. Looking at the dynamics of the way a board or committee changes its sense of role and authority in response to a change in leadership can illumine the discussion. I develop it here in terms of a parish religious education advisory board, but the same dynamics can be applied to diocesan commissions or other types of groups.

Any time we look in on a group, we are coming in somewhere in the middle of the cycle. So we pick up the Religious Education Advisory Board (REAB) for St. Odo the Good Parish at the point of stabilization.

Stabilization

The REAB had been in existence for several years. Started by the former DRE, Martha, the Board of seven to ten members understood itself to be advisory in nature. In the first year or so (during the original period of genesis and growth), there was some tension about decisions that had been made at an REAB meeting being overturned or just forgotten by Martha. But Martha was really clear on her vision for the group and worked to be sure that the vision was understood and embraced by the REAB membership: This group was to be simply an advisory group. Martha set up the agenda and invited comments and suggestions on some of the issues that faced the religious education program. In addition to serving as an advisory group, it was often the members of this group that were asked to do the little extra things that help a program run smoothly. While all of the members were asked to help, most of the tasks were completed by just a couple of people.

In *Spiritlinking Leadership* Donna Markham has an inter-esting discussion concerning the evolution of working groups. The kind of tension that Martha experienced with the REAB is reflective of the move from the "inclusion" phase, where partic-ipants are polite and avoid confrontation, to the "confrontation" phase, where issues of power, authority, and control come to the fore. The final phase is "collaboration," where the insights of the entire group are respected and the members understand them-selves to be colleagues.[4] To stay in one of the first few phases can easily lead to stagnation rather than stability as the group is en-gaged in attending to its inner dynamics rather than addressing the task at hand. Looking back on the REAB in the year or so before Martha left, that certainly seemed to be the case.

Breakdown

There are subtle signs of "breakdown" in any group that is in need of change: attendance is down, energy for new projects or ideas is low, disagreements that had been resolved come up again, new members are hard to find, and those who do come into the group are often isolated or dismissed. That was pretty much the state of things when Martha decided to leave the po-sition at St. Odo's and Mary was hired to take her place.

Dis-integration

For the first several months after Mary arrived, the REAB con-tinued to meet monthly. While in some ways the meetings were similar to the ones that Martha ran, it became increasingly clear that Mary had a different vision for the REAB and for religious education at St. Odo's in general. At times it seemed as though no one was communicating very well at all. Mary asked one of the members to serve as chair of the group, and that wasn't a popular decision. A couple of meetings had to be rescheduled because of conflicts with other parish events. As Mary attempted to set out her vision of the REAB and her hopes for the parish, she was generally greeted with silence or vague acquiescence. Toward the end of her first year, as Mary began to talk about elements of the religious education that she believed were in need of change, many of the members became defensive; a couple went to the pastor to complain. Ultimately, the REAB in that configuration simply fell apart—it lost its center and its vision; it lost its integrity. It dis-integrated.

Note that what dis-integrated at St. Odo's was more than just the REAB, which disbanded because of the challenge of change in the overall understanding of catechesis that Mary and other members of the parish team were setting before them. Often marked by feelings of impending chaos and fear of the future, this phase of dis-integration may be fiercely resisted even by those who acknowledge that change is necessary. We tend to respond to the challenge of dis-integration in a variety of ways. Here I mention four unhelpful ones that were clearly present at St. Odo's that year.

1. Most obvious is *denial*. We simply deny that any serious change is needed. "Really, it's not as bad as you think it is," we might tell one another. "Things are going well enough," a colleague might tell us. "No matter what you do for some people, they are never satisfied," we might think to ourselves.

   The most obvious effect of denial is to turn a blind eye to the fact that breakdown/dis-integration is taking place and needs to take place. A second effect is to silence the people who are pointing out the necessity of change, who are saying this just is not working. Denial serves as a dismissal of those who argue for change.

2. Related to this first negative response is a second, which also denies the breakdown: we spend time simply patching the present. We could have better cate-

chist formation or more meetings with parents, we could have the students come in less often, or more often, or on a different day; or in a different space. These are all incidental changes that usually have little impact on the overall need for substantive change. This reflects an attempt to keep the attention away from the reality of breakdown and the need for a new creation. A dish or plate that is broken can sometimes be glued back together. And if we leave it alone on a shelf there is no problem; but add a little heat or a little pressure and it breaks again.

3. The third kind of reaction acknowledges the reality that the present is no longer working, that we need to see a new vision. But nonetheless it serves to block any real creativity because it places blame. Someone might say, "If the parents would get more involved we wouldn't have the kind of discipline problems we are having." Or "If we had some of the money that is always being spent on the school, it would be possible to do something creative."

This third kind of reaction is a response of defeat and withdrawal: if we could only change something else the breakdown wouldn't be happening; we could continue the way things are.

4. A similar effect is created in the final reaction: rigidity. By becoming more rigid, more structured, we hold back the anxiety that is produced by the impending or present dis-integration. Rigidity is a "circling of the wagons" response that thwarts creativity in the belief that one can safely weather the threat by holding tight to the present model.

These reactions are expressions of resistance. Markham writes:

Resistance in and of itself is neither good nor bad. It is an *unconscious* process of retarding or blocking the process of transformation. No group or individual can withstand unimpeded change. Resistance serves the purpose of allowing an organism to consolidate its gains as it internalizes changes it has undergone.[5]

Let me be clear: resistance in itself is neutral, though unhelpful expressions of resistance, such as those listed above, are negative. All of these reactions have two things in common: (1) they focus on external problems rather than present challenges and opportunities and (2) they are time- and energy-consuming: whether those in leadership react that way or simply have to respond to others who react that way. In either case, such reactions keep the group from its main task, which is setting out an alternative vision and leading into a new future.

FOR YOUR
REFLECTION AND CONVERSATION

1. What elements of this description of the process of and reaction to change corresponded to your experience? Where did you disagree or want to take exception?

2. Where would you place your own catechetical work in this cycle of the process of change? What reactions do you see in yourself or in others?

3. How are you in your own ministry

   • keeping things going so that others don't experience the breakdown?

   • making clear the signs of the need for genesis?

   • supporting others in their positive embracing of the reality of change?

WHAT'S A LEADER TO DO?

How does a leader respond with hope and effectiveness to the process of change and the resistance being expressed on a variety of levels? Resistance in whatever form it takes, when left unchecked, works against the changes being introduced no matter how many people within the institution have affirmed them as necessary and worthy. In the literature that examines this topic, four themes come through repeatedly:[6]

1. *Express with clarity the central vision and conviction of the group.*

In the process of moving from dis-integration to genesis, Mary, the new DRE at St. Odo the Good, spent extensive time talking with people in the parish about their hopes, dreams, and convictions about the life of the parish. She concentrated particularly, though not exclusively, on those committed to the religious education program. From these discussions and her own reflection, she articulated a clear statement of the vision of faith formation and the convictions that support them.

In talking about the nature of conviction, Craig Dykstra writes: "A conviction is something we cannot help believing because, if we did not believe it, we would not be ourselves anymore. In this way we can almost say we are our convictions."[7] Mirroring to a group the convictions and vision that serve as guide and goal for them is an important first step. It is in that context that the discussion of change is rooted.

2. *Speak the truth about the present reality.*

A leader counters the denial and blaming of resistance with a clear articulation of reality, saying clearly, when necessary, "This is not working" and inviting others to name the signs of breakdown and dis-integration that concerns them. While acknowledging the truth can be difficult and painful, it is through this that the motivation for genuine change arises.

3. *Engage as many people as possible in the process of naming the present reality and articulating the path of change.*

At the heart of the learning community is the conviction that all members are called to be actively engaged in learning.[8] That same perspective needs to be in play here as we talk about the process of change: involving as many people as possible, especially those whose voices are not often heard, is crucial to effective change.

Note, however, that an effective leader draws on the insights of the community not simply because it is expedient. From the Christian perspective, we are aware that the Holy Spirit works through all of the members of the community of faith and that gifts have been given to each for the building up of the whole community. It is in drawing on the wisdom of as many persons as possible that renewal can genuinely be effected.

4. *Be ready to let go.*

Back to St. Odo the Good for a moment: One of the most challenging elements of the genesis of a new way of thinking about faith formation and a new role for the REAB was the need to let go of elements and programs that simply did not support the renewed sense of conviction and vision. In many cases these elements had been successful in the past and were considered standard ways in which the parish operated. Many people found letting go of them an admission that the work done in the past had not been worthwhile.

Although Mary as DRE and others on the parish team had been central to the move for change, they too had to let go. They had to let go of what they had thought would be best for the parish in service to the vision and convictions of the whole. Change is often no easier for the leadership than it is for the membership—sometimes it is more difficult!

After a time of experiencing and naming the dis-integration, a *genesis* followed at St. Odo the Good. The REAB was reconceived as a working committee where coordinators of different elements of the parish catechetical endeavor meet monthly for prayer, conversation, and strategizing for the future. The members of the committee served as an essential resource for facilitating change and *growth* at every level of parish life.

LEADERSHIP IN TIME OF CHANGE

Our discussion of change and the way in which we and others respond to—and resist—change serves as an important foundation for the second core topic of the chapter: how we understand the role of leadership. Behind the description of how a leader can effectively deal with change is a theological sense of the place and role of the leader.

As it was important to name our experience of change before launching into a discussion of the theory of change, taking care to engage our experience of leadership is the first step here as well.

Naming Our Experience of Leadership

Reflect on your own experience of leadership—either as a leader yourself or in experiencing the leadership of someone else. Name an event that stands as an example of effective and life-giving leadership; something that you can point to and say "When I think of effective leadership, this is what I mean."

Take time to sink yourself into that situation: Who was involved? What was the setting? What were the dynamics of the situation? What role did you serve? Jot down the basic description of this experience—enough that you can effectively tell a couple of other people about it in a coherent way.

In conversation with others, gather in groups of three; each person takes a turn "chairing" the conversation.

- Briefly state the experience that speaks most clearly to you of the nature of leadership.

- After a brief pause, invite your companions to reflect back to you what they see as the presumptions about leadership underlying your account. You may be surprised by what they say!

- Conclude with observations on your own insights concerning the nature of leadership.

- When each has had a turn, reflect back on the presumptions that were set out. Are there some that all held in common? Are there places where certain characteristics seemed to be seen as essential—without this effective leadership doesn't happen? Be prepared to report that to the full group.[9]

The Leader as Prophet

As we look to the resources of the Christian tradition for insight into the nature of leadership, particularly in time of change, the role and task of the prophets seems to be a good starting point. They, too, have been most active in times of crisis, challenge, and change. How might their understanding of their role give us some insight for the role of leader in the Church today?

In considering the role of the prophet and the voice with which the prophet speaks, we can turn for insight to the lives and times and proclamations of Hebraic prophets. From Moses through Jeremiah and Ezekiel to Jesus of Nazareth, it is possible to explore the task of the prophets and the implications of their work for the vision of prophetic ministry in our own time. While each prophet spoke to his own time and people, there are themes common to all of the prophets that can enhance this discussion of the nature of the prophetic voice.[10]

First, the role of the prophet is both clear and complex: to articulate and nurture a vision of reality that, while running contrary to the contemporary perceptions, is in keeping with the action of God.[11] With intimate knowledge and personal engagement with the plight of the community, the prophet speaks of alternative ways to understand the present and to imagine the future. Whether addressing those in oppression and exile, or those experiencing apparent freedom and contentment, the prophet highlights the contradiction between the present experience and the vision of God.

Second, the insights of the prophets are rooted in their ability to recognize and to name the assumptions that serve as foundations for the status quo. By giving expression to tacitly held presumptions about power and authority, relationships and privilege, the prophet's voice brings to consciousness the underlying forces—many unjust and oppressive—that serve as grounding for maintaining things as they are and have always seemed to be. Making explicit that which has been implicit is a central task and challenge for those giving voice to the prophetic.

In the prophet's task of articulating an alternative view of the present by exposing the generally held presumptions about reality, the third common theme of the prophetic voice comes to light. The prophet speaks not only of a new way to understand the present but of the promise of a new future. Things do not have to be as they are; they cannot remain as they are for those who hear and hearken to the prophet's voice. But the new future is not the result of the prophet's words alone. To claim and nurture the possibility and promise of the prophet's proclamations requires a willingness to enter into a process of letting go and holding on—a process of relinquishment and reclamation.[12] The believer and the community of faith must be willing to let go of the present which they know and, holding on the promise of God's fidelity and love, lay claim to a renewed future set out by the prophet.

Those prophets to the Israelites, major and minor alike, had the ability to recognize the infidelity of the present interpretation of reality, the perceptiveness to articulate the assumptions that served to fix firmly that interpretation, and the imagination to propose a new future and ultimately to convince people of the accuracy and adequacy of their prophetic viewpoint.

Contemporary prophets have these same tasks; in fulfilling them the prophets contribute to the continual renewal of the community of faith.

What's a Prophetic Leader to Do?

How does one gain and speak out of the prophetic vision? How does a catecehtical leader bring the eyes of the prophet to the work of faith formation? That really is the quintessential question for each of us in our apprenticeship to Jesus Christ. While the response of each will vary, I set out here two proposals that are worth attention: First, the prophetic leaders need to attend to their own inner life, and second, they need to hold on to their life preservers as they feel themselves falling out of the raft.

Attend to Your Inner Life

In an important article on leadership, Parker Palmer makes a convincing and challenging case for the absolute necessity for leaders to attend with special care to their inner life. He writes:

> A leader is a person who has an unusual degree of power to project on other people his or her shadow, his or her light. A leader is a person who has an unusual degree of power to create the conditions under which other people must live and move and have their being, conditions that can either be as illuminating as heaven or as shadowy as hell. A leader must take special responsibility for what's going on inside his or her own self, inside his or her consciousness, lest the act of leadership create more harm than good.[13]

Palmer is clear and compelling in his call to recognize the importance of leaders in doing their own inner work, to recognize that there are a variety of influences on their decisions and directions.[14]

Reflecting back to the notion of Mezirow's framework of meaning perspectives and meaning schemas,[15] it is essential that leaders be particularly attentive to distorted meaning perspectives: Those that limit, are exclusive, and fail to account for the variety and diversity of experience.

In the final analysis, Palmer warns us away from the variety of "shadows" that can influence leadership and the lack of light that leadership can cast—fear of chaos, thinking that everything depends on me, lack of trust, fear of failure. And at some level, as we move into times of change—white-water times as Hawkins would say[16]—we are reminded of the second directive to prophetic leaders.

Hold Firmly to Your Life Preserver

In the end we are called to hang on to nothing other than our confidence of God's love expressed in Jesus Christ. As leaders in the Church, that is the life preserver that serves as a firm foundation when the raft is heading for the rocks or rushing through the rapids. We have been gifted to be present in the Church at this time and in this place; we can trust in God's presence now and always.

NOTES

1.   Thomas R. Hawkins, *The Learning Congregation: A New Vision of Leadership* (Louisville, KY: Westminster/John Knox Press, 1997) 19.

2.   Larry Spears, *Reflections on Leadership: How Robert K. Greenleaf's Theory of Servant-Leadership Influenced Today's Top Management Thinkers* (New York: John Wiley & Sons, 1995),19.

3.   Building on the work of Arnold Toynbee, an English historian who died in the late 1800s, Donna Markham proposes the basic outline of this cycle of change in "Psychological Aspects of Change," *Human Development* 5 (fall 1984). However, I don't think she gives enough attention to the period of stability or to the dynamics that contribute to breakdown. In her later writing, particularly *Spiritlinking Leadership: Working Through Resistance to Organizational Change* (New York: Paulist Press, 1998), she explores more closely the relationship among dis-integration, chaos, and resistance.

4.   *Spiritlinking Leadership*, 98–105

5.   *Spiritlinking Leadership*, 24.

6. Several theorists have examined this area. Those I have found particularly helpful include Donna Markham whose main works are cited in the above footnotes. Also Parker Palmer (particularly in *Spirit at Work*, which we will discuss a bit later in the chapter); much of the work in learning organizations deals with the role of the leadership, and indeed all of the members, in facilitating change (Here see the writing of Peter Senge cited in Chapter 4, particularly *The Fifth Discipline Fieldbook: Strategies and Tools for Building a Learning Organization* [New York: Currency, 1994].) Finally, writing in the area of servant-leadership, a term coined and advanced by Robert K. Greenleaf, includes a discussion of the leader's role in supporting the growth and development of the organization.

7. Craig R. Dykstra, *Vision and Character: A Christian Educator's Alternative to Kohlberg* (New York: Paulist Press, 1981), 52.

8. This is discussed in detail in Chapter 4.

9. This is an adaptation of a model of critical reflection on significant experiences proposed by Stephen Brookfield.

10. A resource that has served well the pastoral life of the church is the writing of scripture scholar Walter Brueggemann. With keen insight into the cultural and ecclesial realities that shape and challenge contemporary ministry, Brueggemann delves into the role of the prophets, particularly in the Old Testament, for insight into what it means to speak with a prophetic voice today.

11. This theme comes through clearly in Walter Brueggemann, *The Prophetic Imagination* (Philadelphia: Fortress Press, 1978) as well as *Hopeful Imagination: Prophetic Voices in Exile* (Philadelphia: Fortress Press, 1986).

12. For a development of this idea, see Brueggemann's examination of the role of the prophets in the context of exile. See *Hopeful Imagination*, "Introduction: Exile and the Voice of Hope." For Brueggemann, the role of the prophet in postexilic Israel is to help the people relinquish the old ways of doing things and receive God's power as source of hope.

13. Parker J. Palmer, "Leading from Within: Out of Shadow, into the Light," in *Spirit at Work: Discovering the Spirituality in Leadership*, ed. Jay Alden Conger (San Francisco: Jossey-Bass, 1994), 24–25.

14. This issue of the understanding of the human person that Palmer reflects is an important one to take into account. It reminds us that the way in which we think of ourselves as humans needs to be tempered with a recognition of our sinfulness. Within the Catholic context that is often referred to as Christian realism. Coming from the Protestant perspective, Palmer tends to emphasize human sinfulness more and serves as a helpful reminder of the complexity of human reasoning.

15. See Chapter 3 for this discussion.

16. Thomas R. Hawkins, *The Learning Congregation*.

BIBLIOGRAPHY

Barker, Joel Arthur. *Future Edge: Discovering the New Paradigms of Success.* New York: Morrow, 1992.

Bass, Dorothy C., ed. *Practicing Our Faith: A Way of Life for a Searching People.* San Francisco: Jossey-Bass, 1997.

Birkenholz, Robert J. *Effective Adult Learning.* Danville, IL: Interstate Publishers, 1999.

Bowlby, John. *Attachment and Loss.* 2d ed. New York: Basic Books, 1982.

Boyack, Kenneth. *The New Catholic Evangelization.* New York: Paulist Press, 1992.

Boyd, Robert D., and John M. Dirkx. *Personal Transformations in Small Groups: A Jungian Perspective,* The International Library of Group Psychotherapy and Group Process. London; New York: Routledge, 1991.

Brennan, Patrick J. *Re-Imagining Evangelization: Toward the Reign of God and the Communal Parish.* New York: Crossroad, 1994.

Bringuier, Jean-Claude, and Jean Piaget. *Conversations with Jean Piaget.* Chicago: University of Chicago Press, 1980.

Brookfield, Stephen. *Becoming a Critically Reflective Teacher.* The Jossey-Bass Higher and Adult Education Series. San Francisco: Jossey-Bass, 1995.

_____. *Developing Critical Thinkers: Challenging Adults to Explore Alternative Ways of Thinking and Acting.* San Francisco: Jossey-Bass, 1987.

_____. *Discussion as a Way of Teaching: Tools and Techniques for Democratic Classrooms.* San Francisco: Jossey-Bass, 1995.

_____. *The Skillful Teacher: On Technique, Trust, and Responsiveness in the Classroom.* San Francisco: Jossey-Bass, 1990.

_____. "Using Critical Incidents to Explore Learners' Assumptions." In *Fostering Critical Reflection in Adulthood: A Guide to Transformative and Emancipatory Learning*, edited by Jack Mezirow and Associates. San Francisco: Jossey-Bass, 1990.

Brueggemann, Walter. *Hopeful Imagination: Prophetic Voices in Exile.* Philadelphia: Fortress Press, 1986.

_____. *The Prophetic Imagination.* Philadelphia: Fortress Press, 1978.

Brueggemann, Walter, Sharon Parks, and Thomas H. Groome. *To Act Justly, Love Tenderly, Walk Humbly: An Agenda for Ministers.* New York: Paulist Press, 1986.

Brusselmans, Christiane, James A. O'Donohoe, James W. Fowler, and Antoine Vergote. *Toward Moral and Religious Maturity.* Morristown, NJ: Silver Burdett, 1980.

Burbles, Nicholas, and Suzanne Rice. "Dialogue Across Differences: Continuing the Conversation." *Harvard Educational Review* 61 (1991): 393–416.

Burton, Terence T., and John W. Moran. *The Future-Focused Organization: Complete Organizational Alignment for Breakthrough Results.* Englewood Cliffs, NJ: Prentice-Hall PTR, 1995.

Campbell, Dennis G., and Alban Institute. *Congregations as Learning Communities: Tools for Shaping Your Future.* Bethesda, MD: The Alban Institute, 2000.

Castelli, Jim, and Joseph Gremillion. *The Emerging Parish: The Notre Dame Study of Catholic Life Since Vatican II.* 1st ed. San Francisco: Harper & Row, 1987.

Clark, Janice E. "On Writing, Imagination and Dialogue: A Transformative Experience." In *Transformative Learning in Action: Insight from Practice*, edited by Patricia Cranton. San Francisco: Jossey-Bass, 1997.

Clark, M. Carolyn. "Changing Course: Initiating the Transformational Learning Process." Paper presented at the 34th Annual Adult Education Research Conference, University Park, PA, 1993.

_____. "The Restructuring of Meaning: An Analysis of the Impact of Context on Transformational Learning." Paper presented at the 33d Annual Adult Education Research Conference, Saskatoon, Sask., 1992.

_____. "Transformational Learning." In *An Update on Adult Education Theory*, edited by Patricia Cranton. San Francisco: Jossey-Bass, 1993.

Clark, M. Carolyn, and A. L. Wilson. "Context and Rationality in Mezirow's Theory of Transformational Learning." *Adult Education Quarterly* 41, no. 2 (1991): 75–91.

Coffman, P. M. "Inclusive Language and Perspective Transformation." Paper presented at the 32d Annual Adult Education Research Conference, Norman, OK, 1991.

Collard, Susan, and Michael Law. "The Impact of Critical Social Theory on Adult Education: A Preliminary Evaluation." Paper presented at the 32d Annual Adult Education Research Conference, Norman, OK, 1991.

_____. "The Limits of Perspective Transformation: A Critique of Mezirow's Theory." *Adult Education Quarterly* 39, no. 2 (1989): 99–107.

Congregation for the Clergy. *General Catechetical Directory*, Washington, DC: USCC, 1971.

_____. *General Directory for Catechesis (GDC)*. Washington DC: USCC, 1997.

Connell, Martin, ed. *The Catechetical Documents: A Parish Resource.* Chicago: Liturgy Training Publications, 1996.

Cooper, Gillian. "Freire and Theology." *Studies in the Education of Adults* 27 (1995): 66–78.

Cote, Richard G. *Re-Visioning Mission: The Catholic Church and Culture in Postmodern America*, Isaac Hecker Studies in Religion and American Culture. New York: Paulist Press, 1996.

Courtenay, Bradley C. "Are Psychological Models of Adult Development Still Important for the Practice of Adult Education?" *Adult Education Quarterly* 44 (1994): 145–53.

Cowan, Michael A. "The Sacred Game of Conversation." *Furrow* 44 (1993): 30–34.

Cowan, Michael A., and Bernard Lee. *Conversation, Risk and Conversion: The Inner and Public Life of Small Christian Communities.* Maryknoll, NY: Orbis, 1997.

Cranton, Patricia. *Professional Development as Transformative Learning: New Perspective for Teachers of Adults.* San Francisco: Jossey-Bass, 1996.

_____. *Understanding and Promoting Transformative Learning: A Guide for Educators of Adults.* San Francisco: Jossey-Bass, 1994.

Cunningham, Phyllis. "From Freire to Feminism: The North American Experience of Critical Pedagogy." *Adult Education Quarterly* 42 (1992): 180–92.

_____. "The Social Dimension of Transformative Learning." *PAACE Journal of Lifelong Learning* 7 (1998): 15–28.

Dannefer, D., and M. Perlmutter. "Development as a Multidimensional Process: Individual and Social Constituents." *Human Development* 33 (1990): 108–37.

Darcy-Berube, Françoise. *Religious Education at a Crossroads: Moving on in the Freedom of the Spirit.* New York: Paulist Press, 1995.

Davidson, James, et al. *The Search for Common Ground: What Unites and Divides Catholic Americans.* Huntington, IN: Our Sunday Visitor, 1997.

Dewey, John. *Experience and Education.* New York: Collier, 1938.

Dirkx, John M. "Nurturing Soul in Adult Learning." *NCACE* 74 (1997): 79–88.

_____. "Transformative Learning Theory in the Practice of Adult Education: An Overview." *PAACE Journal of Lifelong Learning* 7 (1998): 1–14.

Dirkx, John, Phyllis Cunningham, Metchild Hart, Jack Mezirow, and Sue Scott. "Conceptions of Transformation in Adult Education: Views of Self, Society and Social Change." In *34th Annual Adult Education Research Conference,* edited by D. Flannery, 254–61. University Park: Pennsylvania State University, 1993.

Dulles, Avery. "John Paul and the New Evangelization." *America,* February 1, 1992.

Dykstra, Craig. "What Is Faith? An Experiment in the Hypothetical Mode." In *Faith Development and Fowler,* edited by Craig R. Dykstra and Sharon Parks. Birmingham, AL: Religious Education Press, 1986.

Dykstra, Craig R. *Growing in the Life of Faith: Education and Christian Practices.* Louisville, KY: Geneva Press, 1999.

_____. *Vision and Character: A Christian Educator's Alternative to Kohlberg.* New York: Paulist Press, 1981.

Dykstra, Craig R., and Sharon Parks. *Faith Development and Fowler.* Birmingham, AL: Religious Education Press, 1986.

English, Leona M. *Mentoring in Religious Education*. Birmingham, AL: Religious Education Press, 1998.

Erikson, Erik H. *Dimensions of a New Identity*. 1st ed. New York: Norton, 1974.

_____. *Gandhi's Truth on the Origins of Militant Nonviolence*. 1st ed. New York: Norton, 1969.

_____. *Identity and the Life Cycle: Selected Papers*, Psychological Issues, V. 1, No. 1. Monograph 1. New York: International Universities Press, 1959.

_____. *Identity, Youth, and Crisis*. 1st ed. New York: W. W. Norton, 1968.

_____. *The Life Cycle Completed, Extended Version with New Chapters on the Ninth Stage of Development by Joan M. Erikson*. New York: Norton, 1997.

Erikson, Erik H., and Huey P. Newton. *In Search of Common Ground: Conversations with Erik H. Erikson and Huey P. Newton*. 1st ed. New York: Norton, 1973.

Ewert, G. "Habermas and Education: A Comprehensive Overview of the Influence of Habermas in Educational Literature." *Review of Education Research* 61 (1991): 345–78.

Flannery, Austin, ed. *Vatican Council II. Constitutions, Decrees, Declarations*. Revised ed. Northport, NY: Costello Publishing, 1996.

Fowler, James W. *Becoming Adult, Becoming Christian: Adult Development and Christian Faith*. San Francisco: Harper & Row, 1984.

_____. *Faithful Change: The Personal and Public Challenges of Postmodern Life*. Nashville, TN: Abingdon, 1996.

_____. *Stages of Faith: The Psychology of Human Development and the Quest for Meaning*. San Francisco: Harper & Row, 1981.

_____. *To See the Kingdom: The Theological Vision of H. Richard Niebuhr*. Lanham, MD: University Press of America, 1985.

_____. *Weaving the New Creation: Stages of Faith and the Public Church*. 1st ed. San Francisco: Harper & Row, 1991.

Fowler, James W., Sam Keen, and Jerome Berryman. *Life Maps: Conversations on the Journey of Faith*. Waco, TX: Word Books, 1978.

Fowler, James W., and Robin W. Lovin. *Trajectories in Faith: Five Life Stories*. Nashville, TN: Abingdon, 1980.

Freire, Paulo. *Pedagogy of the Oppressed*. rev. ed. New York: Continuum, 1993.

Frydman, Bert, Joanne Wyer, Iva M. Wilson, and Peter Senge. *The Power of Collaborative Leadership: Lessons for the Learning Organization*. Woburn, MA: Butterworth-Heinemann, 2000.

Gadamer, Hans-Georg. *Truth and Method*. 2d rev. ed. New York: Continuum, 1999.

Gallagher, Michael Paul. *Clashing Symbols: An Introduction to Faith and Culture*. New York: Paulist Press, 1998.

Gardner, Howard. *Frames of Mind: The Theory of Multiple Intelligences*. New York: Basic Books, 1983.

_____. *Intelligence Reframed: Multiple Intelligences for the 21st Century*. New York: Basic Books, 1999.

Gerard, Glenna, and Linda Teurfs. "Dialogue and Organizational Learning." In *Community Building: Renewing Spirit and Learning*, edited by Kazimierz Gozdz. San Francisco: New Leaders Press, 1995.

Gillen, Marie A., and Maurice C. Taylor. *Adult Religious Education: A Journey of Faith Development*. New York: Paulist Press, 1995.

Gilligan, Carol. *In a Different Voice: Psychological Theory and Women's Development*. Cambridge: Harvard University Press, 1982.

_____. *Mapping the Moral Domain: A Contribution of Women's Thinking to Psychological Theory and Education*. Cambridge: Center for the Study of Gender Education and Human Development Harvard University Graduate School of Education: Distributed by Harvard University Press, 1988.

Gozdz, Kazimierz, ed. *Community Building: Renewing Spirit and Learning*. San Francisco: New Leaders Press, 1995.

Grabove, Valerie. "The Many Facets of Transformative Learning Theory and Practice." In *Transformative Learning in Action: Insights from Practice*, edited by Patricia Cranton. San Francisco: Jossey-Bass, 1997.

Grace, A. P. "Where Critical Postmodern Theory Meets Practice: Working in the Intersection of Instrumental, Social and Cultural Education." *Studies in Continuing Education* 19, no. 1 (1997): 51–70.

Groome, Thomas H. *Christian Religious Education: Sharing Our Story and Vision*. 1st Harper & Row paperback ed. San Francisco: Harper & Row, 1981.

_____. "The Purpose of Christian Catechesis." In *Empowering Catechetical Leaders*, edited by Thomas Groome and Michael Corso. Washington, DC: National Catholic Educational Association, 1999.

_____. *Sharing Faith: A Comprehensive Approach to Religious Education and Pastoral Ministry: The Way of Shared Praxis*. 1st ed. San Francisco: HarperSanFrancisco, 1991.

Gross, Francis L. *Introducing Erik Erikson: An Invitation to His Thinking*. Lanham, MD: University Press of America, 1987.

Harris, Maria. "Completion and Faith Development." In *Faith Development and Fowler*, edited by Craig R. Dykstra and Sharon Parks. Birmingham, AL: Religious Education Press, 1986.

_____. *Fashion Me a People: Curriculum in the Church*. Louisville, KY: Westminster/John Knox, 1989.

Harris, Maria, and Gabriel Moran. *Reshaping Religious Education: Conversations on Contemporary Practice*. Louisville, KY: Westminster/John Knox, 1998.

Hawkins, Thomas R. *The Learning Congregation: A New Vision of Leadership*. Louisville, KY: Westminster/John Knox, 1997.

Hayes, Matthew J. "Public Talk in a Public Church: Developing Political Response-Ability." *The Living Light* 35 (1999): 29–37.

Hooks, Bell. *Teaching to Transgress: Education as the Practice of Freedom*. New York: Routledge, 1994.

Horan, Michael P., and Jane E. Regan. *Good News in New Form: A Companion to the General Directory for Catechesis*. Washington, DC: National Conference of Catechetical Leaders, 1998.

Imel, Susan. *Transformative Learning in Adulthood*. ERIC Digest No. 200, 1998 [cited October 25, 2000]. Available from http://ericacve.org/docgen.asp?tbl=digests&ID=53.

International Council for Catechesis. *Adult Catechesis in the Christian Community: Some Principles and Guidelines; with Discussion Guide*. Washington, DC: United States Catholic Conference, 1992.

Jansen, T., and D. Wildermeersch. "Beyond the Myth of Self-Actualization: Reinventing the Community Perspective of Adult Education." *Adult Education Quarterly* 48, no. 4 (1998): 216–26.

Jarvis, Peter. *Paradoxes of Learning: On Becoming an Individual in Society*. San Francisco: Jossey-Bass, 1992.

_____. *The Practitioner-Researcher: Developing Theory from Practice.* The Jossey-Bass Higher and Adult Education Series. San Francisco: Jossey-Bass, 1999.

Jarvis, Peter, and Nicholas Walters. *Adult Education and Theological Interpretations.* Original ed. Malabar, FL: Krieger, 1993.

John Paul II. *Apostolic Exhortation on the Vocation and the Mission of the Lay Faithful in the Church and in the World (Christifideles Laici). Origins,* February 9, 1989, 561–95.

_____. *Encyclical on Mission Activity (Redemptoris Missio). Origins,* January 31, 1991, 541–68.

Keane, R. "The Doubting Journey: A Learning Process of Self-Transformation." In *Appreciating Adults Learning,* edited by D. and V. Griffin Boud. London: Kogen Page, 1987.

Keefe, James W. *Learning Style Theory and Practice.* Reston, VA: National Association of Secondary School Principals, 1987.

Kegan, Robert. *The Evolving Self: Problem and Process in Human Development.* Cambridge: Harvard University Press, 1982.

_____. *In over Our Heads: The Mental Demands of Modern Life.* Cambridge: Harvard University Press, 1994.

_____. "There the Dance Is: Religious Dimensions of a Developmental Framework." In *Toward Moral and Religious Maturity,* edited by C. Brusselmans. Morristown, NJ: Silver Burdett, 1980.

Kerka, Sandra. *The Learning Organization* [Internet]. ERIC/ACVE, 1995 [cited 2/1 2001]. Available from http://ericacve.org/docgen. asp?tbl=mr&ID=59.

Kohlberg, Lawrence. *Essays on Moral Development.* 1st ed. San Francisco: Harper & Row, 1981.

_____. *The Philosophy of Moral Development: Moral Stages and the Idea of Justice.* 1st ed. Vol. 1 of *Essays on Moral Development.* San Francisco: Harper & Row, 1981.

_____. *The Psychology of Moral Development: The Nature and Validity of Moral Stages.* 1st ed. Vol. 2 of *Essays on Moral Development.* San Francisco: Harper & Row, 1984.

Kolb, David A. *Experiential Learning: Experience as the Source of Learning and Development.* Englewood Cliffs, NJ: Prentice-Hall, 1984.

Lakeland, Paul. *Postmodernity: Christian Identity in a Fragmented Age.* Minneapolis: Fortress Press, 1997.

Land, George, and Beth Jarman. "Beyond Breakpoint: Possibilities for New Community." In *Community Building: Renewing Spirit and Learning,* edited by Kazimierz Gozdz. San Francisco: New Leaders Press, 1995.

Loder, James E. *The Transforming Moment: Understanding Convictional Experiences.* San Francisco: Harper & Row, 1981.

Markham, Donna. "Making Friends with the Dragon: Women's Leadership in a Time of Transformation." *Human Development* 12, Summer (1991): 27–33.

_____. *Spiritlinking Leadership: Working Through Resistance to Organizational Change.* New York: Paulist Press, 1998.

Markham, Donna J. "Psychological Aspects of Change." *Human Development* 5 (Fall 1984): 24–28.

Marsick, Victoria, Jeanne Bitterman, and Ruud van der Veen. "From the Learning Organization to Learning Communities Toward a Learning Society." In *Information Series No. 382.* Columbus, OH: ERIC Clearinghouse on Adult, Career and Vocational Education, 2000.

Marthaler, Bernard. "Catechesis as Conversation." *The Living Light* 27, no. 4 (1991): 309–17.

Mayo, Peter. "Synthesizing Gramsci and Freire: Possibilities for a Theory of Radical Adult Education." *International Journal of Lifelong Education* 113 (1994): 125–48.

Merriam, Sharan B., and Rosemary S. Caffarella. *Learning in Adulthood.* 2d ed. The Jossey-Bass Higher and Adult Education Series. San Francisco: Jossey-Bass, 1999.

Merriam, Sharan B., and M. Carolyn Clark. "Learning from Life Experience: What Makes It Significant?" *International Journal of Lifelong Education* 12, no. 2 (1993): 129–38.

Mezirow, Jack. "Contemporary Paradigms of Learning." *Adult Education Quarterly* 46, no. 3 (1996): 158–72.

_____. *Education for Perspective Transformation: Women's Re-Entry Programs in Community Colleges.* New York: Teacher's College, Columbia University, 1978.

_____. *Learning as Transformation: Critical Perspectives on a Theory in Progress.* The Jossey-Bass Higher and Adult Education Series. San Francisco: Jossey-Bass, 2000.

_____. "On Critical Reflection." *Adult Education Quarterly* 48, no. 3 (1998): 185–98.

_____. "Transformation Theory and Cultural Context: A Reply to Clark and Wilson." *Adult Education Quarterly* 41, no. 3 (1991): 188–92.

_____. "Transformation Theory and Social Action: A Response to Collard and Law." *Adult Education Quarterly* 39 (1989): 169–75.

_____. "Transformation Theory of Adult Learning." In *In Defense of the Lifeworld: Critical Perspectives on Adult Learning*, edited by Michael Welton, 39–70. Albany: State University of New York Press, 1995.

_____. *Transformative Dimensions of Adult Learning.* San Francisco: Jossey-Bass, 1991.

_____. "Transformative Learning: Theory to Practice." In *Transformative Learning in Action: Insights from Practice*, edited by Patricia Cranton, 5–12. San Francisco: Jossey-Bass, 1997.

Moore, Mary Elizabeth. *Education for Continuity and Change: A Model for Christian Religious Education.* Nashville, TN: Abingdon, 1983.

Moran, Gabriel. *Religious Education Development: Images for the Future.* Minneapolis: Winston Press, 1983.

Murphy, Christopher J. "Conversation with Religious Classics: A Shared Interpretation Approach to Religious Education." Ph.D. diss., Boston College, 1997.

NCCB. *Our Hearts Were Burning Within Us: A Pastoral Plan for Adult Faith Formation in the United States (OHWB).* Washington, DC: USCC, 1999.

Neuman, T. P. "Critical Reflective Learning in Leadership Development Context." Ph.D. diss., University of Wisconsin, 1996.

Osborne, Kenan B. *Christian Sacraments in a Postmodern World: A Theology for the Third Millennium.* New York: Paulist Press, 1999.

Palmer, Parker J. *The Active Life: A Spirituality of Work, Creativity, and Caring.* 1st ed. San Francisco: Harper & Row, 1990.

_____. *The Courage to Teach: Exploring the Inner Landscape of a Teacher's Life.* 1st ed. San Francisco: Jossey-Bass, 1998.

_____. "Leading from Within: Out of Shadow, into the Light." In *Spirit at Work: Discovering the Spirituality in Leadership*, edited by Jay Alden Conger. San Francisco: Jossey-Bass, 1994.

_____. *Let Your Life Speak: Listening for the Voice of Vocation.* San Francisco: Jossey-Bass, 2000.

_____. *The Promise of Paradox: A Celebration of Contradictions in the Christian Life.* Notre Dame, IN: Ave Maria Press, 1980.

_____. *To Know as We Are Known: A Spirituality of Education.* 1st ed. San Francisco: Harper & Row, 1983.

Parks, Sharon. *The Critical Years: The Young Adult Search for a Faith to Live By.* 1st ed. San Francisco: Harper & Row, 1986.

Parks, Sharon Daloz. *Big Questions, Worthy Dreams: Mentoring Young Adults in Their Search for Meaning, Purpose, and Faith.* San Francisco: Jossey-Bass, 2000.

Paul VI. *On Evangelization in the Modern World (Evangelii Nuntiandi),* 1975.

Perry, William Graves, and Harvard University. Bureau of Study Counsel. *Forms of Intellectual and Ethical Development in the College Years: A Scheme.* New York: Holt Rinehart and Winston, 1970.

Piaget, Jean. *Play, Dreams, and Imitation in Childhood.* New York: Norton, 1962.

_____. *Six Psychological Studies.* New York: Random House, 1967.

Regan, Jane. "Principles of Catechesis from Ecclesial Documents." In *Empowering Catechetical Leaders,* edited by Thomas Groome and Michael Corso. Washington, DC: United States Catholic Conference, 1999.

_____. "When Is Catechesis of Adults Genuinely Adult?" *The Living Light* 37, no. 1 (2000).

Robertson, Douglas L. "Transformative Learning and Transition Theory: Toward Developing the Ability to Facilitate Insight." *Journal on Excellence in College Teaching* 8, no. 1 (1997): 105–25.

Saavedra, Elizabeth. "Teachers Study Group: Contexts for Transformative Learning and Action." *Theory into Practice* 35, no. 4 (1996): 271–77.

Scherer, James A., and Stephen B. Bevans. *New Directions in Mission and Evangelization.* Maryknoll, NY: Orbis Books, 1992.

Schön, Donald A. *Educating the Reflective Practitioner: Toward a New Design for Teaching and Learning in the Professions.* 1st ed. San Francisco: Jossey-Bass, 1987.

_____. *The Reflective Practitioner: How Professionals Think in Action*. New York: Basic Books, 1983.

Schweitzer, Friedrich, J. A. van der Ven, and James W. Fowler. *Practical Theology: International Perspectives*, Erfahrung und Theologie, Vol. 34. Frankfurt am Main; New York: P. Lang, 1999.

Scott, S. M. "The Grieving Soul in the Transformation Process." In *Transformative Learning in Action: Insight from Practice*, edited by Patricia Cranton. San Francisco: Jossey-Bass, 1997.

Selman, Robert L. *The Growth of Interpersonal Understanding : Developmental and Clinical Analyses*. London; New York: Academic Press, 1980.

Senge, Peter M. "Creating Quality Communities." In *Community Building: Renewing Spirit and Learning*, edited by Kazimierz Gozdz. San Francisco: New Leaders Press, 1995.

_____. *The Fifth Discipline: The Art and Practice of the Learning Organization*. New York: Doubleday/Currency, 1990.

_____. *The Fifth Discipline Fieldbook: Strategies and Tools for Building a Learning Organization*. New York: Currency, 1994.

_____, ed. *Schools That Learn: A Fifth Discipline Fieldbook for Educators, Parents, and Everyone Who Cares About Education*. New York: Doubleday, 2000.

Senge, Peter, Art Keeiner, Charlotte Roberts, Richard Ross, George Roth, and Bryan Smith. *The Dance of Change: The Challenge of Sustaining Momentum in Learning Organizations*. New York: Currency/Doubleday, 1999.

Seymour, Jack L. *Mapping Christian Education: Approaches to Congregational Learning*. Nashville, TN: Abingdon, 1997.

Seymour, Jack L., Margaret Ann Crain, and Joseph V. Crockett. *Educating Christians: The Intersection of Meaning, Learning, and Vocation*. Nashville, TN: Abingdon, 1993.

Seymour, Jack L., and Donald Eugene Miller. *Contemporary Approaches to Christian Education*. Nashville, TN: Abingdon, 1982.

_____. *Theological Approaches to Christian Education*. Nashville, TN: Abingdon, 1990.

Shaw, Susan M. *Storytelling in Religious Education*. Birmingham, AL: Religious Education Press, 1999.

Shor, Ira, and Paulo Freire. "What Is 'Dialogical Method' of Teaching." *Journal of Education* 169, no. 3 (1987): 11–31.

Shorter, Aylward. *Evangelization and Culture.* London: Chapman, 1994.

Spears, Larry C., ed. *Reflection of Leadership: How Robert K. Greenleaf's Theory of Servant-Leadership Influenced Today's Top Management Thinkers.* New York: John Wiley & Sons, 1995.

Swain, Bernard F. *Liberating Leadership: Practical Styles for Pastoral Ministry.* 1st ed. San Francisco: Harper & Row, 1986.

Tarr, Dennis L. "The Strategic Toughness of Servant Leadership." In *Reflection of Leadership: How Robert K. Greenleaf's Theory of Servant-Leadership Influenced Today's Top Management Thinkers,* edited by Larry C. Spears. New York: John Wiley & Sons, 1995.

Taylor, Edward W. "Analyzing Research on Transformative Learning Theory." In *Learning as Transformation: Critical Perspective on a Theory in Progress,* edited by Jack Mezirow, 285–328. San Francisco: Jossey-Bass, 2000.

————. *The Theory and Practice of Transformative Learning: A Critical Review,* Information Series 374. Ohio State University: ERIC Clearinghouse on Adult, Career, and Vocational Education, 1998.

Tennant, M.C. "Life-Span Developmental Psychology and Adult Development: Implications for Adult Learning." *International Journal of Lifelong Education* 9 (1990): 223–35.

————. "Perspective Transformation and Adult Development." *Adult Education Quarterly* 44 (1993): 34–42.

Toffler, Alvin. *Powershift: Knowledge, Wealth, and Violence at the Edge of the Twenty-First Century.* New York: Bantam, 1991.

Tracy, David. *The Analogical Imagination: Christian Theology and the Culture of Pluralism.* New York: Crossroad, 1981.

————. *Blessed Rage for Order, the New Pluralism in Theology.* New York: Seabury Press, 1975.

————. *Plurality and Ambiguity: Hermeneutics, Religion, Hope.* San Francisco: Harper & Row, 1987.

Veiling, Terry. *Living in the Margins: Intentional Communities and the Art of Interpretation.* New York: Crossroad Herder, 1995.

Vella, Jane Kathryn. *Learning to Listen, Learning to Teach: The Power of Dialogue in Educating Adults,* The Jossey-Bass Higher and Adult Education Series. San Francisco: Jossey-Bass, 1994.

_____. *Training Through Dialogue: Promoting Effective Learning and Change with Adults.* 1st ed., The Jossey-Bass Higher and Adult Education Series. San Francisco: Jossey-Bass, 1995.

Warren, Michael. *At This Time, in This Place: The Spirit Embodied in the Local Assembly.* Harrisburg, PA: Trinity Press International, 1999.

_____. *Faith, Culture, and the Worshipping Community.* New York: Paulist Press, 1989.

_____. *Seeing Through the Media: A Religious View of Communications and Cultural Analysis.* Harrisburg, PA: Trinity Press International, 1997.

_____, ed. *Sourcebook for Modern Catechetics.* Winona, MN: Saint Mary's Press, 1983.

Welton, Michael. "Shaking the Foundations: The Critical Turn in Adult Education Theory." *Canadian Journal for the Study of Adult Education* 5 (1991): 21–42.

Westerhoff, John H. *Inner Growth, Outer Change: An Educational Guide to Church Renewal.* New York: Seabury Press, 1979.

_____. *Spiritual Life: The Foundation for Preaching and Teaching.* 1st ed. Louisville, KY: Westminster/John Knox Press, 1994.

_____. *Tomorrow's Church: A Community of Change.* Waco, TX: Word Books, 1976.

_____. *Will Our Children Have Faith?* New York: Seabury Press, 1976.

Whitehead, James D., and Evelyn Eaton Whitehead. *Method in Ministry: Theological Reflection and Christian Ministry.* San Francisco: Harper & Row, 1980.

Wickett, R. E. Y. *How to Use the Learning Covenant in Religious Education: Working with Adults,* Kenosis Series. Birmingham, AL: Religious Education Press, 1999.

Wonacott, Michael E. *The Learning Organization: Theory and Practice* [Internet]. ERIC/ACVE, 2000 [cited February 1, 2001]. Available from http://ericacve.org/docgex.asp?tbl=mr&ID=102.

Yukl, Gary A. *Leadership in Organizations.* 4th ed. Upper Saddle River, NJ: Prentice-Hall, 1998.

INDEX

By the nature of the text, some terms appear throughout: reign of God, adult church, evangelization, conversation, etc. The more significant references to these ubiquitous terms are given here.

225